Word Weaver.
A Prison Tale

By

M. Wray

For Sarah and John

Dedication

For all the men who shared their lives and time and stories with me, for my daughter and son-in-law who goaded me into this writing, for a few fellow former inmates who reminded me of facts not well remembered or forgotten; thank you. I also dedicate this volume to the few friends who stuck with me in my trails and to the millions of people on this side of the razor wire who support their loved ones on the other side of it.

Thanks to Sarah, A.J., and Glen, for assisting me in the proofing and editing of this manuscript. Finally, special thanks to John P. for being a constant sounding board throughout the writing and editing phase of part one. I hope to use you all again in the future...in like manner.

Prologue

Before I begin my prison tale, I must of necessity unblock years of blocked memory and allow myself to dream again. Prison, they say, hardens a person. That much is true. None of us expect to end up there- to be deemed such a danger or monster that society has to put us away for a while, sometimes for life.

The dream we all share- a happy marriage, a beautiful spouse, loving children, a satisfying and successful job or career- are all surrendered at the strike of the hammer. The paradise we deeply desired and sought so hard to create- sometimes with big toe just over the line of what honest folk call 'legal'- turns into a nightmare at worst. At best, an endless purgeless purgatory continues long after incarceration. The residual mental and emotional shame, pain, and anguish many times dealt with by self-abuse using alcohol and drugs.

Nevertheless, this weaver's words are not so much about the painful realities of prison life, of injustice or of justice served. It is about some of the decent men I knew during my years of internment, of their dreams, hopes, and fears, of their peculiar conditions, and like soldiers serving in a hostile place, of their desperate desire to stay connected- to stay in love with their sweethearts back home, and for them to stay in love with them, too.

Make no mistake; prison is a hostile place. No matter how your incarcerated loved one lies about it, it is a place filled with many nefarious and threatening and dangerous characters, some of whom you will meet herein. As I said, this account is not about them, so much as, it is about the decent loving man taken from you and sent to that cankerous timeless void.

As is true with any injustice or hardship thrust upon you or that you have thrust upon yourself, prison works every day making you whatever you will 'be' once your sentence has been served. For most, me included, 'bitter' is the word that often comes to mind about the effect prison has on a person. It leaves a man bitter.

There is little attempt at rehabilitation, no redemption, nor is there any opportunity afforded to make restitution. As I said, prison is a gnawing purgatory that lingers, at least in heart, long after you have left there, but enough about that. Prison afforded me, a college-educated man, a unique experience and opportunity.

Because of my education, after serving months slopping hash in the food line, I was sought out and made a G.E.D. tutor. That one shift in reality gave me a safe and true prison identity. You see, the one-fourth of the prison population at that time that did not have a high school diploma was court-mandated to get a G.E.D. Suddenly the threatening intimidating characters who would try to rob me of my 'lunch money' now needed me and tagged me by a different epithet.

My old assigned designation of 'fish' was transformed into one of endearment, Old-Gangster. From that moment on not one nefarious character hardly messed with me. I was accepted and protected.

That title, however insanely humorous I found it to be in prison and thereafter, is not the title I took away from the experience with pride and humility. In the course of my six daily hours of tutoring, something profound happened. I discovered that I had a talent for writing- a quite serendipitous discovery I assure you- and not just any kind of writing.

One day, a strapping handsome willfully illiterate young man asked me to write a letter for him to his sweetheart using fancy poetic-type words. After a few more such letters, he was so impressed that he asked me to write a short love story including him and his sweetheart. As word spread, so did requests for similar letters and stories. From that day on, that man and others crowned me *Word Weaver*. This is the story as I remember it.

Part One:
The Vinegar

Randy

Randy was twenty-five when I met him- a white southern Missouri farm boy- handsome, muscular. You know the type- athletic, blonde hair, blue eyes, oozing charisma out every pore. Endowed with common sense, he deemed school not worth the time or effort and dropped out just at the beginning of the eleventh grade.

The reasons: horses, a girl, and the 'ideal' that his sense of humor was equal to the task of getting him through any of the difficulties he might face in the adult world. Besides, his girlfriend would continue in school and be the backup brains when needed.

Although some did, Randy found it ridiculous and downright unpatriotic to try to disguise, divorce, or distance himself from his agrarian roots and humble upbringing. In fact, he was downright proud of it. It was the rest of the nation that had funny accents and peculiar ways. In his way of thinkin', he was the very definition of an American. He was, after all, from the state of the most 'American' of all Americans- *Huck Finn and Tom Sawyer.*

How he thought he could get away with it in this day and time, I will never know. (Although I am assured many do get away with it.) You see, Randy's family farm was not in the best of financial circumstances. It was mortgaged from hoof-to-hilt, as he described it. So being an avid fan of the 'wacki-tabacci' himself, at a friend's high-urging, he decided to become the 'American' of all American ideals, an entrepreneur. That got him and his friend ten years.

When I first met him in G.E.D. class, a Biblical reference immediately came to mind. Here was a boy "sick of love"- as the Song of Solomon in the King James Version puts it. He was the most forlorn and mournful fella I ever had the privilege to meet and know.

Back home, Randy had left his sweetheart from since middle school. Millie was her name. They were true bookends. From head-to-toe, she seemed, from her pictures and letters, to be the female version of him.

Like most men in those circumstances, Randy feared that Millie would soon grow weary of his absence, lose hope and find someone else. Millie tried to put out of her mind the myriad stories offered by some of Randy's friends who had 'been there'- stories about younger men in those desperate circumstances who find the wiles and charms of an effeminate 'cellie' more than a little appealing.

As I tutored Randy for a while in English Grammar, he became frustrated at the slow pace of his ability to grasp or learn it. After all, why can't ya 'rite thangs like ya think 'em, and spell thangs like ya say 'em? He then confessed his sad dilemma.

The confession did not come in the classroom. It was rendered on the yard sitting on the bleachers of the baseball field. Soon, the heartfelt confession gave way to heart-warmed tears. Randy felt utterly inadequate to communicate in written words what he had physically and emotionally communicated to Millie for many years. He needed an amanuensis, a scribe of the soul.

It was at that most human meeting that that most southern boy 'begged' without apology for help. He needed a secretary to pen his most private intimate thoughts and feelings for his beloved back home- using poetic words woven from the bare threads of a soul laid bare. Chosen for this auspicious honor against my will and better judgment, I did protest my inadequacies.

Randy had made up his mind. I was the best and possibly the only candidate for the job. He thought of me as sensitive, caring, and knowledgeable about matters of the heart. What gave him that 'ideal' I will never know.

The most solemn commission was paid in the 'coin of the realm'- a pack of premium cigarettes for each very-long letter. Although I did not smoke, I did accept a can of chili or a box of snack cakes for my modest fee. I protested that I did not want or need them. But Randy was an honorable man. An invaluable service was being rendered and must be repaid.

It wasn't long after he began receiving amorous return letters from Millie, that Randy pulled me aside and on those very bleachers said, "Man, you know what you are? You're a fuckin' word weaver." He then begged from me another literary favor, a love story.

Within a year of Randy's incarceration, his folks had lost the family farm. Millie had to leave the doublewide trailer and move back home- to a horse ranch with her folks. The pressure on all, as you can imagine, was unbearable. There were many sleepless nights on both sides of the razor wire fence.

Millie and her parents did visit once a month and accepted expensive collect calls twice a week. Randy's parents visited every so often- whenever one of their older sons could bring them. It was during one of the visits with Millie that Randy's quelled guilt and usually controlled selfless-protective nature erupted. He verbally questioned their 'until death do us part' relationship.

More than once, he pleaded for Millie to divorce his "sorry-ass" and to marry a man who could give her all he had promised. More than a few tears were shed during that visit. COs (Correctional Officers; prison guards) had to warn them against touching.

He was not allowed to touch her. Randy wasn't allowed to touch even a hair of his beloved during their visits, and there was no such thing as a 'conjugal' at that prison. How could this brokenhearted man *touch* his brokenhearted wife? How could he offer comfort to her in their distress? Visits and phone calls seemed not enough. Letters were welcome and somewhat comforting but seemed equally inadequate.

Randy and Millie wanted and needed to rewrite their story. He was determined, though all the demons of hell tried to prevent him, that he would make love to his woman again. He would share intimate details of their lives with his prison 'pen' and create words so worthy and worlds so magically and powerfully present that she would feel his presence with her again.

As you can imagine, no living human being would have envied me. I did not covet the idea of getting my ass 'whooped' by a forlorn farm boy being daily tested by his 'he-she' cellie, not to mention being tested by the consuming pain of missing his sweetheart- and for your information, Randy did get testy more than a few times.

The first few attempts at the love stories were too short on personal and intimate details and failed miserably. At the time I thought, "Discretion is the greater part of valor." It is, after all, very difficult and sometimes embarrassing to capture the affections of two strangers by a yet, stranger-stranger.

Nevertheless, dismissing unspoken fears, embracing the human heart, offering a listening ear, I penned several intimate love stories of Randy and Millie. That's when the trouble started. (The reader will find the first chapter of their fantasy love story in part two entitled, The Boy Monk and the Acolyte. Their more factual love story is also there at the end entitled, The Palomino Picnic.)

I cautioned Randy on more than one occasion to keep our agreement secret and to keep my writing of his love letters and love stories private. However, the very fact that we met two hours daily walking the track or sitting on the bleachers talking put targets on our backs. We began to be the objects of unwanted scrutiny, gossip, and lies.

Randy was a hugger. Many times his joy in reading his love's response letters unbound him from all the constraints of prison etiquette, and he translated his exuberant thanks into a hearty bear hug. This was simply 'not done'. As I fondly recall it now, how could he keep our secret when the love stories and letters had brought so much comfort, peace and joy to him and to his sweetheart? Short answer: He could not. However, that wasn't how we were found out.

His cellie read some of the letters and stories composed before Randy mailed them while he was with me laying the groundwork for more letters. This had a less than desirable effect, as you can imagine. The love letters and stories meant for Millie were consumed first by 'Allie', and he fell deeply in love with Randy.

Brendon, my Romeo

When I first met Brendon, we were buck-naked standing in one of the many lines of about twenty-five or thirty naked men. I was close behind him and had a good view of his shoulder blades. We had surrendered our civilian clothes and dignity, and with them our identity at the door. We were processed at the Fulton Reception and Diagnostic Center. Very soon after, our bodies were deloused. We then rinsed off as a CO, a correctional officer, looked on.

After partially drying ourselves, we stood in line to get orange jumpers or coveralls- no underwear. I remember the concrete floor feeling very cold to my feet. We all shivered in those cold dark rooms and embraced the thin, small, almost hand-towels as if they were full-size blankets or quilts. They were the only source of relief and dignity offered before we were assigned numbers in place of names and *unflattering* photos were taken for I.D. badges.

What, how did we feel at the time? I think I can speak for all present that day. We did not feel humiliation, fear, anger, or insanely, a sense of camaraderie. Like the elderly, we all felt what our feet felt. Numb. 'Culture Shock' comes to mind but does not quite capture the experience. Be assured, later on, some of us did feel humiliated, fearful- bitter.

They say that trying circumstances bring out the best in you. That extreme trial brings the true leaders to the forefront. While the rest of us stood around in our orange coveralls, the COs handed the last two pair to the last two inmates. Cruel does not begin to describe what I witnessed that day. Some of the other 'previous quests' laughed and mocked at what they saw. One young man did not.

Purposefully, the COs picked the largest man, who happened to be a return guest- black as night, muscular as a Mr. Universe, yet humble and quiet- and gave him the smallest pair of coveralls. At the same time, they gave the largest pair of coveralls to the much smaller white man. As the smaller, older, obviously arthritic man tried with difficulty to roll up his pair of coveralls to fit him, the larger younger man tried to 'slip into' his coveralls, tearing out the crotch in the process.

The COs then had the men stand facing each other in the middle of the room- as if it were a sporting arena- strip, and exchange coveralls. The immediate observation by all was that the 6' 4" young black man was hung like the proverbial horse. The 5' 4" almost elderly white man was, let us say, not.

As men laughed and pointed with the COs, it was apparent to those with a conscience that the small man was blushing shame, as he quickly put on his coveralls. The black man's eyes and demeanor exhibited sincere sympathy and compassion. That is when Brendon stood up.

The boy was the very definition of courage. He rebuked all around him for their sneers and jeers and shot a look of menacing displeasure at the COs. Surprisingly, those around the boy did quiet themselves. The COs ordered everyone to line up to get their bedding and toiletries, before marching them to their housing units. Uniforms would be issued later in the day. At that instant, Brendon walked over and gave a side-hug to his new friend.

Carl, trying to hold the ripped crotch of his coveralls together, looked up at the 6'2" frame and whispered a thank you. Henry, the black man, offered his hand in friendship to Carl and to Brendon and apologized for ripping out the crotch of the coveralls. Then and there, I knew I had to get to know those remarkable men.

I must be clear on this point. Brendon was a small-town, well-educated, white boy of the tender age of seventeen. He was incarcerated for getting his fourteen-year-old girlfriend pregnant. Although both his and her parents volunteered to help raise the baby until the lovebirds were old enough to marry, the state of Missouri, in its wisdom at that time, made no distinction or provision for 'Romeo and Juliet' type 'crimes'.

Brendon, like many other young men back then, was charged as an adult offender with several counts of statutory rape and sentenced to ten years. He further was ordered to complete the MOSOP- Missouri Sexual Offender Program. Forever, upon his release from prison, he would be regarded as a loving hard-working husband, father...and a registered sex offender.

This is going to sound ludicrous, but it is true. By law, Brendon could not be transferred to an 'adult' prison until his eighteenth birthday. Therefore, he remained at the Reception and Diagnostic Center for several months- until he turned eighteen. What is so ludicrous about that is this: The diagnostic center was not filled with minors. It was filled with adults- many, hardened criminals.

At the diagnostic and reception center, the inmates were housed like cattle in the very overcrowded housing units and in Quonset hut tents on the yard. Yes, there were cells- tiny two-man cells. Fifty sets of bunk beds sat in both the lower TV/recreation bays and on the upper tiers along the walls of each wing.

The older men like me, or younger men with disabilities, mental disorders, or of obvious homosexual orientation, resided in the cells. The younger men resided in bunk beds in the open bay. (I envied their freedom of movement in the open wing. Those in cells were only allowed out one hour a day for recreation, to shower, and to go to and from the chow hall at meal times.)

To accommodate those living in the cells, a few young men- the most hyper and likely to cause trouble- were given the paid job of 'Walkman'. It was their job to listen for celled-inmates yelling, and to fetch for them pencils, stationary and envelopes, library books, or to get them ice in small plastic bags slid under the doors. They also served as postmen of sorts for back and forth communication with other celled-inmates.

The other young men were not allowed to loiter outside the cell doors, but did peek in and beg for cigarettes or for a word from time to time. That's how I got to know Brendon. He was immediately made a Walkman.

Brendon never asked for my help writing letters or love stories. But he did bend my ear to listen to his sad tale. I entertained him with corny jokes and one time sat for several hours in my cell with a sheet over my body. He would yell, "Hey Ghost, you need any ice?" I would reply that departed souls did not need ice. He would respond, "They do if they're in hell, brother." At that, realizing that I was in a sort of hell, I took the ice.

Our conversations mainly took place during our quick meals. We lined up and marched to the chow hall. There, we sat where we pleased as long as we ate our meals in twenty-minutes or less. The walk back to the housing unit was leisurely and good for a five-minute chat.

It was during those six weeks of meals and walks that I got to know Brendon and Henry. Carl stayed mostly to himself in his cell.

Brendon was, and I am sure now is the nicest person you would ever want to meet. However, incarceration tends to reduce a person to a frazzle of his former self- boredom, cellies, and COs tend to wear the most saintly of souls down. It was not long before Brendon found it hard to render respect to the men in uniform. He made it almost a sport to taunt them, ending with him cussing them out for ignoring the many injustices he witnessed.

The boy found himself in the *hole* a few times, as did I. Being a non-smoker, by written policy, I was not to be assigned a cell with a smoker. Ignoring the policy and common decency, the COs assigned me to a three-pack-a-day man about ten years my senior who came with an added bonus- he coughed all night long.

We ultimately got into a fistfight, but it was not about his smoking. I ended up in the hole at the same time Brendon did, and we shared side-by-side cells for about a week. I found him quite entertaining and resourceful, especially in the hole.

Brendon did not go immediately to the Farmington Correctional Center (FCC) to begin his sentence and the MOSOP. Considered a *gladiator,* on his eighteenth birthday he was shipped to Boonville- where young aggressive hotheaded men are incarcerated. I would not see him again until the end of my fourth year of incarceration. (Now, I must jump ahead and describe that meeting with the young gladiator. I caution the more genteel reader here to avert your eyes and skip this part of the story.)

At FCC, visitation usually takes place on weekends. Visitors are searched before entering the visitation room. Inmates are strip-searched and cavity-searched coming and going. Both A-side and B-side inmates share the same large room and times of visitation. It is at these meetings that they may lean over to a nearby table and greet other inmates they may not have seen for a while.

My parents came for their one and only visit, bringing my children. Brendon had been transferred in and resided in temporary housing in five-house on A-side. I had just been transferred to the A-side to two-house, but did not know he was there.

We met, I think providentially, in the 'dressing' room after our visits. (Inmates were required to strip off their old dingy worn-thin gray uniforms and wear crisp clean white shirts and gray dress pants during their visits. The powers-that-be wanted us to look nice for our relatives or lawyers. After our visits, we were then required to return these fineries.)

Not having a Type-A personality, I obediently and without comment stripped off my clothes and underwear, showed my tongue and teeth and ears, showed my pits, raised my modest ball sack, bent over and pulled my cheeks to reveal that I did not have any hidden contraband in any orifice of my body. Handed my yard uniform, I moved to the side to get dressed. That is when Brendon came in.

If you have ever seen a female Missouri stripper at a club that sells alcoholic beverages, then you will get my meaning. I am not saying that I have ever had the privilege to visit one. Nevertheless, word of mouth is sufficient, by proxy, to appreciate the experience.

For those uninitiated...by law, Missouri strippers working at an establishment that serves liquor may not be completely nude. They must wear pasty-tassels over their nipples and some manner of thong to cover their crotch area. Across the river in East St. Louis, Illinois, one may enjoy alcohol and full-nude entertainment, legally. More about the peculiarity of some Missouri laws, later.

Brendon stripped down to his skivvies. He then jerked them off laughing heartily. Let's just say that I and the two COs who witnessed his prominence of manhood for the first time were quite impressed. It was like seeing a white version of Henry. Let me further state that few men can easily do what he did that day. I am not quite sure what consequences followed, but I am sure that Brendon was, at the least, after that display, barred from visits for a month or two.

Naked as a jaybird, Brendon began gyrations of the body in a way that caused his long flaccid penis to twirl not unlike the pasty-tassels on the nipples of a Missouri stripper. In fact, I think he would have put them to shame. When directed to bend over and spread 'em, he more than willingly did so.

Moving his ample ball sack to one side, he said, "Let me just probe myself to prove there's no contraband in my anal-port." At that very moment, Brendon proved that some men can indeed 'violate' themselves, at least flaccidly.

Laughing deliriously, and thankful to a merciful God that I was granted the privilege to witness a display of such vulgar protestation, I was ordered to exit not yet having put on my sneakers. Those had to be put on outside.

Just before I exited, Brendon filled his large hands with his ball sack, leaned out and said, "You boys caught me red-handed. I do have contraband within my body. But I'm going to need some help getting it out. Could either of you fine gentlemen spare a lubed-hand or better, a warm mouth to get my pecker hard to pump it out?"

Regretfully, that was the last time I saw Brendon. Nevertheless, I shall never forget him. He was a stubborn Missouri mule who refused to be broken or tamed, and he is the one man I met in prison whom I hope never changes. Surely, he is reunited with his love by now and has sired many children by her. He is surely a success in whatever career he has chosen, especially if he has chosen to be a stripper.

Why bring up Brendon? Surely, the reader is aware of the male models used for the covers of romance novels. Let's just say that some of the men I wrote for were less than perfect specimens of the male gender. Most of the men were average like me and not like Brendon. Writing many of the love letters and love stories several months after I met him, Brendon was the template 'Romeo' I had in mind.

A few words about the realities on the 'Yard'

As soon as the new inmate steps off the bus onto the prison yard, he is the target of scrutiny and taunting by some of the resident inmates. Fresh meat or *fish* has arrived. *They* not you, determine your status and level of acceptance. They determine if you arrive with 'street-cred'.

You must keep your 'shit' packed tight at all times, and you must always watch your back and find others to hang with who will also watch your back.

The greatest threats on the yard in pecking order are pimps, drug-dealers, gangstas, the COs who consort with the above, and moneylenders. Usually, the pimps and drug-dealers are the moneylenders, but each house and wing did have a 'store' man. (Storemen and their cellies buy their limit at the commissary and loan one item for two or three in return.)

Cardinal rule #1: Do not borrow money; do not get indebted to anyone.
Cardinal rule #2: You cannot trust just anyone to watch your back.

The Scam: Especially for younger men, within a few hours or days of your arrival, a man will approach you claiming that he or another inmate that he represents has bought you. They will demand money 'paid back' or demand sexual services- for you to prostitute yourself, or for you to be a mule or a fall guy for them. (As I recall, the going rate for a fish back then was two-hundred dollars. That is a huge debt to pay off at the beginning of your prison time.)

Your choices:

1) Immediately, beat the crap out of the man who says he or another inmate owns you. (This will send both of you to the hole for a while, but will show that you keep your 'shit' packed tight.)

2) Put yourself in ADSEG- Administrative Segregation (Protective Custody- that was in one-house on A-side at FCC). It is the last resort for most. Nevertheless, men have been known to get shanked in there, as well.

3) Pay (on the down-low) someone to beat up or shank the one who is threatening you, or arrange for him to be involved in a few yard fights, so he will be transferred to another prison. (You pay 'long-timers' for this service- men who have extended or life sentences.)

Be aware, however, that he, your threat, will still have remaining partners on the yard and maybe in your housing unit who will still want to do you harm. Not to mention that you have indebted yourself to a criminal 'so hard' that he shanks for a price. You will of necessity need to join a gang or buy protection.

4) You can give-in and daily, weekly and monthly pay off your never-ending debt to your pimp through prostitution, thuggery, being a fall guy or lackey, or performing other services depending upon your skill set. Be aware that your 'threat' may sell your 'contract' at will to another pimp or gangsta.

5) If you have the balls and the brains and the street-cred, challenge the pimp, beat his ass and take his boys and business.

There are no loners in prison…although it appears so. "No man is an island. We are all part of the continent." The fish must join a gang or a group for protection. He may join church groups or clubs, but those types usually do not watch your back and surely do not back you up in a 'dust-up'.

All inmates understand that the first part of the process of watching your back is having a cellie you can trust. It sometimes takes weeks or months to accomplish this through a caseworker. The second part of the process is presence. You must *not* be seen on the yard as a loner. You must be seen with homies.

Groups may be defined artificially, racially, or be an extension of 'the hood'. The artificial groups are the ones created, organized and run by the pimps and drug-dealers. The predominant racial ones in most prisons are Whites (Arian Brotherhood), Blacks, and Hispanics.

The gangs from 'the hood' might be, as I saw, the Crips, the Bloods, Black Gangsta Disciples, or other lesser known street gangs, that are just as present, just as dangerous. They are recognized- as gang members are recognized on the outside- by defining tattoos, colors, and graffiti. Gang members are forbidden from displaying their colors or *sign* in prison- not much you can do about the tattoos.

More could be said about the sociology of the groups and gangs in prison and the group dynamics behind them. However, I think the reader has enough information to understand this word weaver's next account. It involves my experience with my first prison cellie.

Anonymous

The name of my first cellie must remain anonymous. You see, he got over twenty years for the manufacture and distribution of methamphetamines. He arrived with immediate 'street-cred' and quickly tried to establish himself and align himself with those involved in the prison's drug trade.

For the first few days, I did not understand or grasp how dangerous he was or could be, or the target immediately put on my back as his cellie. (Why he was placed in two-house and not in four-house, remains a mystery to me.) However, that is not the reason he must remain anonymous. It has to do with 'the code'.

Arriving in a Department of Corrections bus, twenty inmates wearing orange coveralls descended the steps to the jeers and taunts of the residents. 'Fresh meat' has been delivered. After unshackling and being handed small paper bags containing our possessions, Henry urged me aside and nodded in a general direction. Something was happening that we were not meant to see. In what should have been a blind spot, an inmate was exchanging two cartons of premium cigarettes with a CO for a plastic bag filled with a green substance. At least that is how it appeared to me.

The uninitiated might think that the inmate was paying the CO for smuggling pot into the prison. That is what I thought, too. Henry explained that the CO was the 'mule'.

The CO had access to both A-side and B-side of the 'camp'. He was simply facilitating an exchange. I found out later that exchanges were daily made in the school. Tutors had access to A-Side and B-side inmates and some were 'mules'. (The real way a corrupt CO or other prison staff was paid: The prison drug-dealer directed his people on the outside to pay cash or drugs or something else he or she might want in exchange for the smuggling services rendered.)

During our walk across the A-side ball field toward our housing units, Henry made me an offer I could not refuse. No one in his or her right mind was going to mess with Henry. Although I was middle age, I was seen for what I was- a novice, green, an easy mark, a fish. I had no street-cred, and surely could not invent it on the spot with enough gravitas to convince anyone otherwise.

If I paid Henry two cartons of premium cigarettes a month, he would offer his protection. I agreed to the terms and had a friend on the outside send enough money to my prison account to cover the expense for three months. As an 'alpha', Henry would reside on the A-side in four-house with the more aggressive violent offenders- usually repeat offenders.

Designated a 'sigma', I was not viewed as aggressive or threatening. Because I was a 'first-timer', I was assigned a cell on the A-side in one of the four wings of two-house. Later on, I would be transferred to the sigma house on B-side, seven-house.

My cellie introduced himself by throwing his belongings on the top bunk and assigning me to the bottom. I was more than pleased with the arrangement but nodded my benign acquiescence. Anonymous was white, married with small children, twenty-six, about five-ten in height and a quiet sort of fellow. We sat shackled beside each other during our silent bus ride- first driving to the oldest working prison west of the

Mississippi River at the time, The Walls, in Jefferson City. There we dropped off a few men then headed to Farmington.

During my professional days, I had taken part in many seminars about one thing or another. My cellie, upon our first 'open wing' introduced me to a very different kind of seminar. It was truly revelatory.

When a CO in the elevated glass pod that is visible from all four wings announces, "open wing," (usually in the evenings) the cell doors are electronically unlocked...pop, pop, pop, and so on. Men are free to roam from room to room, use the showers, do whatever they care to do. My cellie and his partners held meetings.

No more than four men are allowed in a cell at a given time during 'open wing', so I had to vacate the premises at times. It gave me an opportunity to make new friends and for my cellie to make connections, establish partners, and make a lot of money.

During the times I was present, I overheard several seminars on how to make LSD, Meth, and Ecstasy at home and how to grow marijuana hydroponically in a basement or garage. My cellie was a very knowledgeable man...at least about those things, and he was very good at math. Of course, I was only allowed to listen in upon pain of death...thus, adherence to the code.

About three nights into my stay at FCC, my cellie forced me awake by squeezing my neck to the point that I choked and almost blacked out. To be exact, he pulled me from my lower berth by the neck, thrust me against a wall, and choked me. I was informed at that early stage in our association, "What is said or done in the cell *stays in the cell*." The only conversation more sacred was between a man and his God.

I expressed gratitude for learning the lesson on keeping the code 'this way' rather than by learning it 'the hard way'. A few days later my cellie calmly disclosed that knowing and abiding by the code was mandatory, but that he had been 'under the influence' of crack cocaine when he endeavored to teach it to me- his attempt at an apology.

The reason I bring up Anonymous is this: you hear that common young men go to prison most of the time for committing stupid nonviolent crimes. This was true I think for 40% of the men I knew in prison. They started out as decent good men- loving husbands and fathers.

Years later they left prison hardened criminals well versed in mugging, armed robbery, the making and distributing of illegal drugs, forgery, etc., and like Anonymous, become repeat offenders and frequent guests of the state. Most lose their sense of self-worth along with their family and direction. It is the overwhelming reality of the American system of justice.

For my three months with Anonymous, I worked in the kitchen, as do all newbies. My talks with my cellie and other inmates did cause me to question my long-held and naively sacred view of the Missouri and American systems of justice. The one thing I took away from those relationships and conversations was a Great Awakening. It was through Anonymous and his partners that I began to understand the toll taken on a man and his family due to prolonged incarceration- not to mention the toll and cost to society and the nation at large. I will speak more about that later.

Oh, you want to know more about what happened after the choking incident.

I had a talk with Henry and he had a talk with Anonymous. Reaching a mutual understanding, there was no more talk of 'contracts' or threats of shanking me on the yard. However, I eventually had to pay a few lifers through Henry to provoke a few fights with my cellie on the yard.

You see, I had to get rid of my cellie- to have him shipped out- because he suffered from paranoid delusions, and at times saw me as an undercover cop. I was not going to take the chance of violence against my person again from my crack-head cellie or from one of his partners. The unexpected result of arranging the fights on the yard was that I began to gain street-cred. I was a man who 'kept his shit packed tight'.

Transferred to Boonville, I asked my cellie to say hello to Brendon for me. To this day, I wonder if Anonymous ever knew that I was the one who blindsided him.

Inadvertently, I also gained dubious respect from the drug-dealers on the yard that Anonymous was positioning himself to compete with. This was a truly unexpected bonus for me. I do not think the drug-dealers ever protected me; they did not owe me anything. Regardless, I continued to watch my back every moment I was out of my cell.

A clarifying word about my relationship with Henry: At the time, I did not know why he took to me. We had little interaction outside of a few words here and there. He never claimed that he 'owned' me. He was a repeat-offender, a 'long-timer'. I was a fish. (Before leaving FCC, I came to understand that he needed 'currency' upon his arrival to pay *the* Old-G a token of respect. More about that at the end of part one.)

When threatened by a pimp or someone else, I simply stated that I 'belonged' to Henry. However, I really didn't. I paid him a few cartons of premium cigarettes for 'insurance' for three or so months, until I became a tutor. He never bothered me or asked me for more or for anything beyond our initial agreement. He was kind of like a dark guardian angel.

A Brief word about fights on the yard

You might think that a fight is a fight is a fight, that all fights are the same and for the same reason. They are not...at least on the yard. Let me clarify what I mean. If you really have a score to settle, if you really hate someone, you attack them, maybe even blindside them, but not on the yard.

Every fight I saw on the yard was a choreographed altercation. It was usually two gangstas publically displaying their 'street-cred'. They were displaying their manhood; that they kept their shit tight. They were broadcasting that they were not owned and would not be owned by anyone. (That is not the same as saying that they were not in a gang- that they were not *controlled* by someone else or by someone else's agenda.)

Here is the peculiar thing about two gangstas fighting on the yard: It usually lasts no more than two or three minutes, leaving both men with a few bruises on the face and maybe a bloody noise or lip. It is like watching two deer bucks charging and locking horns, tussling a bit, withdrawing, and charging again. Here is the most interesting thing about it. The fights always occur at designated times and places with a CO a few feet away.

In other words, the fight is held close to a man in uniform with a radio who immediately calls for other COs to join him- running as fast as they can to the scene of the crime- in order to separate the men and haul them to the hole (The hole was in five-house on A-side, as was temporary housing.) There the offenders would cool off- giving them a week's vacation- before eventually returning to the yard.

The fight is a staged safe altercation. There is only the appearance of being a 'bad-ass'. Upon their return to the yard, both men regarded and respected as 'men'. They are not considered 'fish' again.

Many might presume the fight to be an initiation into a gang or a group. This is not so. As on the outside, those rites of initiation are felonious in nature. They usually involve shanking a deadbeat that will not pay his debt or shanking a fish that resists turning tricks for his pimp.

As I said, a true fight, the settling of grievances or scores, usually takes place in private- in a cell or in a blind spot. The bruises and blood explained by, "slipping in the shower."

The exception to the rule: occasionally a man lets his grievances, vexations, and frustrations build up. We see this on the outside of the razor wire from time to time, do we not? It is the same in prison, minus the alcohol.

Sometimes a man cannot take it anymore. After receiving a 'Dear John' letter or after being informed that he cannot attend his dad's funeral because he is a sex offender, who has not yet taken or passed the appropriate therapeutic classes to be allowed even in shackles and under guard on the street like other labeled violent offenders, a spontaneous combustion does take place. Outside of race-related riots, these, to me, seem to be the most dangerous and unpredictable altercations in prison.

Let's see...I've introduced Randy, Henry, Brendon, and Anonymous. I think we need to jump ahead a few months and talk about how I became a G.E.D. tutor. That immediately brings Dwight to mind. Lord, have mercy on me!

Conscripted to be a tutor; Dwight

One of the constants of the stagnancy of prison life is movement. Men are transferred all the time. Without warning, you are ordered to "pack your shit" and transferred from cell to cell, house to house, A-side to B-side, or to another prison. That includes tutors.

While slinging hash in the chow hall making about $7.00 stipend for my 120 hours of work per month, I received a letter from the principal of the G.E.D. school. He had lost several tutors during the time of the return of the "Texas Men," which the reader will find discussed later, through transfers and was seeking college-educated men or men with high school diplomas to become tutors.

At the interview, I was administered the tests men must past to earn their G.E.D. diploma. I had not studied Algebra or Geometry since college, but I had a good memory. I passed in the mid-ninety-percentile and was offered a job earning the top state stipend of $25.00 a month! In other words, I worked the same hours but made almost four times the salary in stipend.

Each classroom in the schoolhouse had round and rectangular tables seating in total twelve to twenty men. Each classroom had a teacher and three or four G.E.D. tutors. (I say each classroom had a teacher. In truth, they were licensed, but some acted more like room monitors. The tutors did most of the real teaching. The teachers did the testing.) Assigned to a smaller classroom with about twelve men, at first I felt awkward, but eventually fell into a routine and enjoyed the experience very much.

The added bonus of the job was that it was a clean job in a well air-conditioned and heated building. (The cells were not air-conditioned – only the CO observation pods were. Nor were the cells heated very well in the winter. Perhaps that is why they say that prison, like politics, makes strange bedfellows.)

Dwight was one of my regulars from four-house, an alpha. He was about as common as a cold and just as hard to shake off. He was, in fact, clingy. However, he had a good sense of humor, which I think he thought more than compensated for his lack of common sense.

Like so many men enjoying their twenties and thirties in prison, Dwight spent part of his free time in the gym weightlifting, or playing basketball or volleyball. When the weather warmed, he tanned, jogged, played handball, basketball or baseball on the yard. Dwight was tall, thick with muscles, sported long dishwater blonde hair that he usually tied in a ponytail, and was quite handsome.

The thing I always found odd about men like him, was that they feigned to dislike and disdain homosexuals. They pointed at them, laughed at them, told jokes about them, pushed them around, but worked hard to make themselves more and more appealing to them. Many went out of their way to get a gay man as a cellie. The point being, many young men do not give up sex while incarcerated. They adapt, as do some middle-age men.

Dwight came to G.E.D. class every morning after breakfast as horny as hell. I have never seen a man in his mid-twenties act more like a middle school boy. To put it out there and not beat around the bush, he did something quite disconcerting on a regular basis, while I was trying to tutor him, that was not conducive to or appropriate in a learning environment.

The teacher assigned to the classroom was a retired elementary school teacher of advanced years, declining health, limited mobility, and quite obese. Let's just say that her days as a 'looker' were well-past. I personally expected her to fall and break a hip or die right there in her chair from a stroke or a heart attack at any time. (I learned years later that she did exactly that- died of a heart attack right there in the classroom. I count that as hearsay.)

To this day, I do not comprehend what I witnessed from Dwight; it was very strange behavior. From our table about eight feet from the teacher's desk, he would masturbate through his thin gray pants all the while saying, "Man, I'd like to tap that," describing the woman's unseen anatomy as if he had knowledge of a personal nature. (He would describe how he would roll up her layers of fat to "tap" that.)

Lucky for him and unlucky for me, the teacher took quite a few naps and never took notice of his bizarre behavior. I had never heard of a fetish for an old obese lady before. Dwight's behavior made me wonder if he was simply desperate for a woman, or if he had a true mental disorder. (I guess it is possible. If a man can be attracted to and desire sex with a corpse, anything is possible.)

A few times the roving CO came unannounced into the classroom and almost caught Dwight indulging his fantasy. More than a few times each morning, I encouraged him to get a bathroom pass and take care of his business in private. That is not to say that he took care of his business alone.

Sometimes Dwight would have a rendezvous of sorts with one of the gay students from another classroom more than happy to service him. Of course, if caught, it would mean a month in the hole for both of them and consequently slow down the earning of their G.E.D. This happened quite frequently, in fact.

Human beings are sexual creatures and creatures of habit. Suppression of sexual desires tends to cause men, especially younger men, to become cranky and ill tempered. They express that ill-temper in a variety of negative ways from provoking fights, to using vulgar language, to destruction of property, to raping the unwilling. (You see a lot of that in prison, or at least hear it after 'lights out' in the cellblock, the wing.)

Sometimes the sounds are frightening. More frightening, the Correctional Officers many times ignore the cries for help. I personally know of a few gangbangs that took place during open wing, free time. During one instance, a boy refused to turn tricks for the man who bought him. He expected at the worst to be beat up on the yard or in the gym, so he avoided those places. He was gang raped in his cell, several men taking turns.

It is hard to yell for help when you are unconscious. After his cellie left to go to the library, instead of pulling his door shut and locking it, the boy left it ajar. He did not realize that his so-called 'daddy' had partners or paid thugs in the wing. Grabbed and knocked unconscious, he was gang raped.

Most men had gone to the yard. The ones who remained in cells nearby surely were aware of the attack and heard the initial cry for help but ignored it. What happens in the cell stays in the cell. That boy ended up in ADSEG.

The common cries occur during the nights between 'count times' after lights-out. Every two hours or so COs walk the wings and shine flashlights in faces through the steel mesh portals of the doors to make sure everyone is accounted for. During those between times, the gay couples and the straight ones with 'willing' cellmates enjoy conjugal bliss. As you can imagine, some men are quite noisy in their amorous and ardent lovemaking. I often thought that the gay men were loud on purpose- a form of advertising.

Everyone knows what is going-down, and who they are going down with or on. It is understood. It is a reality of prison life. Most of the men who enjoy this type of arrangement leave prison and return to their spouses or marry new ones. It is never disclosed or confessed. What happens in the cell stays in the cell.

A word about privacy: Cells are cramped. Quarters are close. Anyone at any time can either look in on you, or during open wing, walk in on you. Some men are modest. Some just want some "fucking alone time". Some need cover to get a tattoo. This is accomplished by using lookouts or temporary privacy curtains.

A privacy curtain is made by tying shoelaces together to make a sort of clothesline and throwing a bed sheet over it. The line is tied to a bedpost and then to the door portal or some other fixture depending on what kind of privacy you or you and your cellie desire.

If, during open wing, you visit a partner and find his door locked and a sheet hanging from under the top bunk mattress shielding the bottom bunk, it is understood. Your 'friend' is pleasuring himself or is having sex with someone. You turn and walk away and do not speak of it.

Most privacy curtains are used because men just want to take a dump without someone watching. I have seen privacy curtains of two sheets- one blocking the view from the door, the other blocking the view from the rest of the cell- from the cellie. (The reader must understand that cells have concrete floors and ceilings, cinderblock walls, steel bunk beds with thin foam mattresses, and metal desks bolted to the floor, as is the one seat. The sink and toilet are stainless steel and located right by the door. Also, one small window opens out for ventilation- in larger cells, two.)

Some readers are surely wondering, 'why don't the men masturbate in the shower.' At FCC, at least, there were three shower stalls in the bay area of each wing or cellblock. The showers boasted small yellow or green plastic shower curtains that covered the area from the chest to the knees of most men.

The showers were visible to the COs in the glass-enclosed pod. Since you never knew when female COs might be present in the pod, if you were seen masturbating, it was a write-up offense and could get you a month or more in the hole. No inmate wanted to risk their job, if they had a good-paying one, or lose their cell if they had a good cellie- not to mention that offense going on their permanent record.

Contrary to popular opinion, condoms are not available at least in Missouri prisons. Oddly, men diagnosed with HIV or AIDS are awakened during the wee hours of the morning by their doors being popped open. Because of privacy laws, the men diagnosed with H.I.V. (about 1% of the total prison population at that time) cannot be disclosed to the other thousand residents of the correctional facility. Therefore, the only way to tell if the person you want to have sex with or are having sex with might have a communicable or deadly disease, is if you or one of your partners are privy to that man's comings and goings in the dead of night to the prison infirmary. Enough said, back to Dwight.

I introduced the reader to Dwight because he was not only a challenge for the tutor, he represented, possibly to some extreme, many of the men I wrote love letters and love stories for in prison. Many men had paramours. Some paid for house calls and had sex in their cells, in the gym or school, or at other discrete locations.

I knew of one inmate who worked in the kitchen and many times directed to work late by his supervisor from the 'outside'. It was later discovered that he was having sex with her in the pantry- she was fired. After his release from prison, they shacked-up.

Dwight was in that category. A particularly 'fine' female CO worked during the evening shift for several months. At times, she would patrol during open wing and enter the various cells, as did the male COs. At the time, I had a cellie in his late twenties. He was fit, toned, and handsome.

While I reclined in my bottom bunk watching my TV, the female CO would lean against the bunk bed with her arms crossed over the top bunk, flirting with my cellie. I got an eyeful. Her ample bosom was close enough to... well, enough about that. There is a point to this.

Dwight fell in love with the very same female CO. They began correspondence through a third party on the outside. (He would mail his letters to her girlfriend's address. She would write him back using an alias.) Dwight still used the services of gay boys on a regular basis during that time, but he buckled down, stopped his undertable manmeat massages and worked hard to earn his G.E.D.

Dwight also used my services, and we collaborated in the writing of many love letters and a few love stories, as well. Before his release, Dwight's lover quit her job at the prison, and upon his release, they married. She was the only woman I wrote love letters to whom I had actually met in prison. The only woman I knew from a bottom bunk view.

Gabriel, Gabriella

Gabriel, Allen-Allie, and Danny-Danielle were the three most prominent prostitutes I knew on the yard. Gabriel and Allen were white. Danny was black. Whereas Allie and Danielle were chatty, flirtatious, and flamboyant, Gabriel was reserved and all business. He was a pimp, and they were two of his girls.

Gabriella, even in her early thirties was stunning. Having in mind that the majority of men at FCC were in their early twenties to mid-thirties- most fit and handsome- when one man stuck out, it was quite an accomplishment. Gabriel was like the regimental royal canons used during the Renaissance and post Renaissance periods- a cold, hard, well-crafted, polished, exact, decoratively ornate, beautiful, deadly work of art.

From Greek stock, Gabriella was about five-foot-eight, had long thick flowing black hair, olive-green eyes and a tanned, shaved sculpted body. When wearing a halter-top exposing her defined cleavage and short-shorts that accented her bubble-butt, in makeup and lipstick, she caused even the most heterosexual of men to stop in lust to stare. She was charming, beautiful, and one of the most dangerous men on the yard.

Introduced to prison life at the tender age of sixteen, Gabriel was serving twenty years for aggravated assault and robbery- the first two years served in a juvenile correction facility. When he first arrived in adult prison, he was 'bought', refused his pimp, and gang raped more than a few times before he had a change of mind and heart. The rapes were the catalyst that began the alchemy of his transformation. From the cocoon of a frightened silly cocky teenage boy-toy, he emerged a fearful (to be feared), muscular, shit-packed-tight, cold-as-steel, no-nonsense, and all-about-business pimp.

My first awareness of Gabriel was on the yard. I had glanced at him in drag a few times. He lived with the most aggressive inmates in six-house on B-side. Walking back from the library to seven-house, I witnessed him beat a man bloody and senseless to the ground behind the bleachers where he proceeded to kick him. It took about a minute for its execution. He was a powerful puncher and an even more powerful kicker.

Separated by twenty feet of open air, I looked down immediately and walked on to my housing unit. Gabriel paused to stare at me. I glanced at him for a brief moment and walked quickly to my housing unit. He left the man on the ground and returned to his house.

A CO was yelling over the loud speakers, "The yard is closed! The yard is closed! Return to your housing units for count time."

Gabriel's timing for beating the man could not have been better. The yard was practically empty with a few men walking swiftly to their houses as if they were iron filings drawn by magnets.

Days after that encounter I could not help but notice that Gabriel seated himself on a bench near my housing unit and stared at me coming and going from the school. He was sending a message. I immediately contacted Henry who by that time also resided in six-house. Gabriel wanted a meeting. A sit down arranged. That only cost me two packs of premium cigarettes.

The meeting:

"You're that tutor that writes the letters. You know who I am?"

"Yes sir, I do. It is a privilege to meet you."

"Most wouldn't say so." Gabriel paused to scrutinize me. It seemed like an eternity. He continued.

"Henry says you pack your shit tight, that you can be trusted."

"Yes sir, that's right."

"Henry's word is good enough for me. I don't need yours. Do you know why I called you to a sit-down?"

"No sir, I don't."

"You don't have to call me 'sir'. Only my girls call me that. I hear some of the men in the school call you 'Old-G'. You know what that means?" Gabriel's tone was one of angry irritation.

"Yes sir," I humbly answered.

"You know you ain't one."

"Yes sir, I do know that."

Gabriel shook his head and grinned- a response I did not expect or think him capable.

"You do know that in my house there is the *real* 'Old-G'. You think I'm a bad-ass? You don't want to meet him. And you sure as hell don't want him to call you to a sit-down."

"No sir, I don't." Gabriel smiled again. At that point, I wondered if he was affording me the privilege to breathe.

"We'll call you 'Old-G' with a little 'g'. How's that suit you?"

"I'd be more comfortable if you called me by my given name."

"No."

"May I ask you a question?"

"If you want to take the risk of getting the shit kicked out of you, feel free." Gabriel said this with a cold dead intimidating stare.

I paused a minute to study the man's eyes. At that point, I felt we were becoming friends.

"You've talked to Henry, so I don't think this meeting is about you making sure that I'm not a narc. So, why are we meeting?"

Gabriel leaned forward on the bench searching in my eyes for my soul. His facial expression and demeanor suddenly went as gray as the uniforms we both were wearing.

"I wasn't always like this, you know."

I remained silent. I expected a 'cards close to the vest' confession was about to be given- probably for the first time in many years.

"I'll tell you my story sometime. For now, I wonder if you would do me a favor."

Hearing the word 'favor' in that context instantly chilled my blood. I am the wrong man if you are looking for a fall guy to shank someone. That is what I thought at that instant. Guys like Gabriel don't ask for normal favors. It is a word loaded down with debt, debts never paid. I would do 'the favor' for this powerbroker-pimp and incur a greater debt than he owed me- another reality of prison.

"What favor?" I asked in anxious whisper.

"This is just between you and me. If I hear it's got out, your ass is mine. Understand?"

"I understand, Gabriel, and I respect you too much to betray your confidences. What's the favor?"

(At this point, the word 'surreal' came to mind.)

"I had a lover. We shared a cell for many years. He just got released a few months back. He said he'd wait for me, but I've maybe got another 'nickel' to walk down before they hand me my papers.

"I'm not illiterate. I got my G.E.D. years ago. I've got money."

"I'd never ask you for money. My payment would be your friendship, Gabriel. What's the favor?"

At that point, Gabriel asked me to assist him in writing love letters to his lover on the outside. This required me reading his lover's letters to him and working with him to respond to them. A dangerous tightrope he asked me to walk; nevertheless, I did walk it.

We became friends, of sorts. Little did I realize, but the writing of the letters was only a test for what was to come- his real reason for wanting to get acquainted with me. He also gave me a warning for my artist, my 'rose' man.

"Earl's been your cellie in seven-house for what, three months?"

"Yeah, he has."

"He's become quite the entrepreneur. Did you know he's branching out?"

"I know he's started making cards and necklaces and doing portraits for guys."

"Old-g, there's one reality your partner hasn't considered- being a player costs. Making any kind of money on the yard draws attention

"He's about to move out and start charging you more for the roses. Old-G is about to call him to a sit-down. Earl hasn't paid the tax.

"You don't know any of this, and you need to let nature take its course. Understand?"

"Old-G isn't going to put out a contract on him, is he?"

"It hasn't got to that yet. Earl is a player. He'll know the score and he *will* comply. If not..." Gabriel shrugged, got up and walked away.

"Thanks for the heads-up, Gabriel."

Out with Earl, in with Santiago

A player is the salesman of all salesmen. He drips charisma, is manipulative at all times, has no street-cred, and bullshits his way out of most, if not all of his dilemmas. Earl was the best I had ever seen. To me, his player side was humorous. It was funny watching him sell his 'snake-oil' remedies as well as his legitimate artwork and jewelry.

Earl was a card shark, and while we were cellies he made a lot of money (cigarettes mainly) doing card tricks. Another part of his personality I also found to be quite humorous- after hearing a very funny joke or anecdote, off the top of his head he would try to make up and tell a funnier one. They always fell flat, but we all laughed anyway, as would he.

Above all, Earl was, on the outside, a ladies' man. He was the kind of man who could charm the panties off a woman before she acknowledged that they were on their first date.

We still keep in touch to this day. Earl does construction-type work and since his release from prison has lived rent-free with one woman after another. He has talked a few of them into buying him a car. Sadly, though he is entertaining, he tends to pathologically lie- a defense mechanism developed while being raised in foster homes. You have to know that about him and that he usually has good but self-serving intentions, to be his friend.

After Gabriel's warning, I confronted Earl about his secret plans. He denied them at first. Then, after I threw a full mug of tea at him, which shattered on the wall behind him, he admitted his plans and duplicity. It was not the fact that I had found out about his plans to move out and overcharge me for his artwork that made him angry at that moment. He wanted to know *where* I found the 'balls' to confront him and how the knowledge of his plans had come to me.

Once I swore him to secrecy and confessed, the fear of the prison Godfather, Old-G, took hold of him. Earl immediately went into 'player' crisis mode. Within twenty-four hours, he moved out.

Straight from spending three months in the hole came Santiago. He was an alpha from six-house and the leader of the remnants of a Hispanic gang. He was a long-timer, tattooed from head-to-toe, tall, thin, muscled, toned, and deeply tanned. He had the weathered face of a man who had lived a rough life. He was housed 'temporarily' in my cell until a bed opened up in six-house or four-house. He was also a heavy smoker...my salvation.

It is against prison policy to house an alpha with a sigma. It is also against prison policy to house a smoker with a non-smoker unless both inmates request it. So, why was Santiago assigned my cell?

To this day, I wonder if Earl had anything to do with it. He had his alliances, his partners. (He threatened that he could get moved out within twenty-four hours; he did, and that he had 'pull' with the COs and the caseworker to make my life a living hell, if I ever crossed him.)

Looking back, I wonder how much Earl feared me at that moment in time. He had known about my agreement and association with Henry. Now, I was also aligned with the most powerful pimp on the yard, Gabriel, who was partner with the Godfather of the yard,

Old-G. Back to Santiago, yet another odd tale to tell. (I apologize to the reader if I use the word 'odd' or 'surreal' continually to describe people and events. Truly, prison is a very odd and surreal place with many odd people. I am not saying that I am not more than a little bit odd myself.)

Living two days and one night with Santiago was not as I imagined it would be. With trepidation, I tell the tale. You would think that sharing a cell with a drug-dealing leader of a gang well known for their shankings would be a simple matter of, "shut up, and do what you are told." He appeared friendly. Three months in solitary confinement for possession of a shank had rendered him 'chatty'.

Santiago talked about his *familia*, his homies, his charges, and his years in prison. He then asked me about mine- not much to tell. Suffering from sinusitis, I took the risk of asking him to do what I had asked Earl, a smoker, to do. "Please stand by the portal of the door or by the window and blow your smoke out." He did so cordially and without complaint. It seemed that we were going to get along just fine, true amigos. Then the night came and with it... lights-out.

Modesty forbids me from going into this next account in graphic detail. For the more prurient reader, I am sure you can fill in the blanks with imagined details undisclosed. After lights-out Santiago, the leader of the 'shanking' gang, asked me for 'a favor'. It was not the favor you would readily expect an alpha to ask of a sigma. It was not the kind of favor you would expect a dangerous gangsta to ask of a fish, but it was equally unnerving.

Before lights-out, Santiago asked me to exchange bunks with him. He required the bottom bunk. I saw no impropriety in the request, yielded it up graciously, and took my repose above him.

Several quiet minutes passed, quiet except for the occasional coughing or low playing radio you hear in the wing at that time of night. The CO came round and shined his light in our faces. It would be at least two hours before he came by again.

The strangest thing about what happened next is not what happened next. As I reflect upon it, I find it strange that it did not happen more than once during my years in prison. You would think that having a new cellie every three to six months, and moving from A-side to B-side and back again several times in the course of those years that this would have happened more often. However, this was the only time I found myself in that awkward untenable position.

Why did Santiago politely demand the bottom bunk?
As he called for me in the dimly lit cell, I looked down at him. He was on his knees with his torso lying over his bunk. I honestly thought he was in prayer. He did sport a Catholic rosary around his neck. Upon his request, I found myself suddenly praying.

"Cellie, have you ever fucked a bitch in the ass?"

"No, can't say that I have. My ex barely allowed me access to her vagina." (Nervous laugh from the top bunk)

"Have you ever fucked a man in the ass?"

"No, I honestly haven't." (Choked response)

"I love to get fucked in the ass. I want you to fuck me."

(Praying time ends, begging time begins.)

Deciding to be proactive and not passive, I hopped off the bed, sat on the shitter, patted Santiago on the shoulder and said, "Brother, I can't. I just can't." He responded by pulling down his shorts revealing his bare, no doubt well-used ass.

"Just dry-hump and pretend to fuck me."

(Unspoken prayers intensify. 'This man could kill me without blinking.')

"I'm sorry. Santiago, I'm so sorry. Maybe I could talk to Gabriel (name-dropper) and get one of his boys for you."

I began to cry. I was acting but the tears were genuine. I was a nervous wreck. If any empathy was left at all in Santiago's soul, tears surely would pull it out. My cellie pulled up his shorts and kneeling by me gave me a side hug. That was the second most surreal moment of the night.

"It's okay brother. I've been in the solitary three months, and I miss fucking, you know. I meant no disrespect."

At that moment, I returned to my bunk and Santiago lit a cigarette and smoked it in the middle of the room, blowing the smoke in my face. His smoking continued in bed for a while thereafter.

"You tell anybody about this and you are *muerto*; understand?" Santiago's tone was an angry tone. His true feelings became clear.

"I understand. I respect you, brother. I would never betray your confidence. What happens in the cell stays in the cell."

He got up, stood by my bunk and nodded, "Damn right it does."

Santiago blew smoke in my face again then threw his filtered cigarette into the toilet. I got the message- both of them. That spent cig could have been my head. He could just as easily extinguish me.

The next morning I made a beeline to the caseworker's office and protested that a smoker had been assigned to my cell, not to mention an alpha that had gone to the hole countless times for aggression. I played the 'I'm calling my lawyer, lawsuit card' making sure that I did not say that I felt threatened by Santiago. Luckily, an inmate from my wing had transferred out that very morning and a bed on the top walk was open. I moved in right after lunch.

It was a corner cell, a bigger cell with two windows. My new cellie was a non-smoker who happened to be an excellent artist. (No need for Earl anymore) Santiago was shipped to Cross Roads a few days later. God does answer prayers.

A note about what happened between Santiago and me. I think even the 'uninitiated' can call up enough imagination to understand that all associations in prison all agreements are 'tit for tat'. Had I been inclined to 'dry-hump' my cellie, the next act of the play would have been him 'dry-humping' me, and it would not have stopped there. He had clearly stated his intentions.

Santiago was a man of honor, a man of the code. Though he was the gangsta, the alpha male, and could have easily rendered me compliant, he graciously offered me his backside before asking me to give up mine.

Every favor, like every debt in prison must be repaid with something of equal or greater value. I paid my unspoken debt the next day with a carton of premium cigarettes- rendering respect to one due respect. (FYI, the price for sex with a 'yard girl' was usually two packs of premium cigarettes.) Thank God, Santiago was an honorable man, and for my friends on the outside who sent me a few bucks every month, or the outcome and this story would have been far different and surely never written.

Jerome

It was not the first teardrop tattoo I had seen. A few men had them at the diagnostic center. The Old-G of six-house had two. Santiago had three. Jerome was an African-American man from 'the Projects' of Kansas City, Missouri. He had one. The difference between the men: Old-G and Santiago wore theirs like a badge of honor; Jerome had 'given his life to Jesus' on the inside and was ashamed of his.

For the uninitiated, each tear represents a person you have killed or a member of your gang or perhaps a family member- many times the same thing- who died during your incarceration. For Jerome, the tear represented an innocent teenage boy he gunned down- part of his initiation into a gang. He was a BGD, a Black Gangsta Disciple, and had the 'tats' or 'ink' to prove it.

Once in a gang, like the mafia, you are in for life- Jesus or no Jesus. So, the unwilling and converted are still expected to hang with their homies and follow orders. They certainly do not have the luxury of hanging with members of other gangs. I think you are beginning to see Jerome's peculiar situation.

His peculiar condition, immediately recognized by me, as I had 'been there' myself, was that he was, like most of the men in prison G.E.D. classes, functionally illiterate. Whether the man is a white redneck from the Boot Heel, a black from the projects (Ghetto), or a Hispanic with limited English, the problem is the same and the treatment is the same.

Jerome had been in G.E.D. classes for five years and continually failed to get his diploma. Why? The teachers and principal and powers-that-be were thinking that it was intentional, because he liked staying in the air-conditioned building in the summer and in the heat during the winter. It was obvious that he suffered from test anxiety.

There was also another factor. Jerome feared transfer and early release from prison without help on the outside, without a place to go. He could not return to his hood.

The remedy for his peculiar condition, to me, was simple. Help him get over his test anxiety, inform the teachers that he was an 'auditory learner' and accommodate for that condition, increase his vocabulary, and give him a goal that would keep him six hours a day in the temperature-controlled building. After all, who better to be a tutor?

Just a word about my story: I graduated high school at the bottom of my class. Earning the lowest score possible on the A.C.T., I started college courses the fall after my high school graduation. Immediately, I began to drown in a sea of endless D's and F's. An English prof came to my rescue.

After taking a battery of tests, it became clear that I graduated from high school and entered college with a fifth-grade reading level and an even poorer vocabulary. I was functionally illiterate. I could spend several pages going over the cause and point fingers, but I shall not at this time. I would rather get to the prescription offered by my professor.

My professor was a Harvard graduate, but that had nothing to do with the remedy he offered for my deficiencies. First, he recommended that I drop out of college immediately in order to save myself from more embarrassment and frustration, and so I could get reimbursed some of the money I had spent on tuition. Second, he prescribed that I memorize two college-level words per day- their spelling, definition, and usage- and that I study an English Grammar textbook that he offered *gratis.*

Taking his advice and the book, I became a dropout, enlisted in the U.S. Naval Reserve, and spent my year of active duty learning about a thousand vocabulary words and studying English Grammar. Once out, I enrolled in a private college that offered a remedial course in English. This was not an easy class.

Upon entering the classroom, one observed that the four walls were chalkboards. For the next twelve months, minus holidays, my fellow functional illiterates and I learned to diagram sentences. We began with simple sentences containing a simple subject and predicate. We moved on to compound then to complex sentences.

We ended up diagraming long sentences that would be divided into seven or eight sentences in normal usage. Along the way, we encountered strange creatures with strange names such as 'gerund' and 'verbal'.

My peculiar background, as you can see, made me uniquely qualified to tutor prison inmates from various backgrounds. In two years of personal and private remedial education, I advanced from a fifth-grade reading level to that of college level. Along the way, I had an epiphany. I did not suffer from retardation. I did not have a learning disability. I was not born stupid.

The other side of the coin- the positive side- I was an academic failure all those years because of my limited vocabulary. Once I had the vocabulary, every subject was my proverbial oyster. When I enrolled again in college, I was no longer the failing clueless student. I understood what I was reading, and I could write about each subject intelligently; people and professors understood what I wrote. After four years, I graduated *cum laude*.

Jerome, after a year of learning college-level vocabulary and proper English Grammar and punctuation, earned his G.E.D. and shortly thereafter became a tutor using the methods I had introduced.

During that year, I assisted him in writing letters. This introduced me to another peculiar aspect of prison life and a pastime of many prisoners- writing pen pals. Jerome discovered in some magazine the names and addresses of women desiring to correspond with men in prison.

Let me pause here to exhale and take a moment for forlorn and regretful memory. Regardless of how saintly the aspiration of the man in prison, he still is...to some degree a...criminal. He goes in warped and comes out more warped or warped, shall we say...differently, with or without Jesus, Allah, Jehovah, or Buddha. (I am not questioning the reformative power of religion here. I am inferring that some felons adopt religion temporarily while incarcerated because attending religious services is one of the factors considered for early parole.)

Your basic felon is by very nature pathological. He is also by nature or nurture, or lack thereof, manipulative. Whether it is due to piss-poor-protoplasm or piss-poor-parenting, or from being raised piss-poor, there is a bent in the thinking and nature of a criminal. Jerome suffered from this malady.

It took several months, but I accidentally discovered that Jerome was using his increasing word-weaving skills to write forlorn creatures forlorn love letters begging for money. He also decided to include a few homosexual men in his pen pal correspondence- talk about a player. Suddenly, the several pairs of new sport shoes and Kansas City Royals jerseys and sweats he donned were not a mystery. He had procured, through deceit, several amorous sugar mommas and sugar daddies.

My daddy used to say, "You put an uneducated man who steals a watermelon in prison, and he'll come out and steal a boxcar full of watermelons." The prison experience proves the truth of it. Not in all cases, but in many, with a 'higher skill set' a 'higher class' of criminal is produced. As I remarked earlier about my first cellie, he held seminars teaching how to manufacture and distribute illegal drugs. Law enforcement officials must always be sharpening their skills to catch the criminal with the higher skill set.

Sadly, I had to modify my association with Jerome- no more assistance in writing love letters. I thought he was writing to one woman. He simply used the originals as templates, copied them, and sent them to several women and a few men.

I was deeply offended by, what he called 'surviving'. I called it manipulation and deceit. His actions were unchristian and unethical. Like my friend Earl, I would imagine that Jerome left prison and became a 'kept' man by a 'sugar momma' to some degree or other.

"All hope abandon ye who enter here"

This next account should come at the end, for it occurred during my last weeks at FCC, before I was transferred to a level-two camp, Church Farm. It is the hardest account to tell. Thinking of it leaves me nauseous, ill. Therefore, I wisely or unwisely put it here in the middle of my story.

The above chapter title is a quote from Dante's *Inferno*. It is the 'welcome mat' if you will, of the gates of hell. That 'greeting' captures the immediate gut feeling I had as I entered my last cell and met my last cellie at FCC. The choking, the fear of rape, the fear of getting shanked or drowned in a toilet, pale in comparison to the anxious dread I lived in every waking moment in my last cell.

Do not take me wrong. I am not sitting in judgment of the man. I truly believe in redemption, restoration, reformation- a second chance. However, I am also equally aware, as is society to some degree, that some are irredeemable.

Some people are not able or willing to be or even cognizant that they need to be reformed- perhaps because they know deep down that they cannot be. We label these characters psychopaths, predators- monsters. They are the Charles Mansons or Adolf Hitlers or Joseph Stalins or Lizzie Bordens or John Wayne Gacys we do not allow our minds to think on without revulsion and repudiation.

There is a sea of difference between being an acquaintance and being someone's cellie, especially if he is a psychopath. Psychopaths, true predators, assume that you are like them, and that you *like them*, because there is nothing wrong with them. They see themselves as different, for sure, but to them that is not the same as being opposite, diametrically opposed, deviant, evil-thoroughly corrupt.

Saying all that, it is very difficult, even for mental health professionals, to gage the level of a man's deviance. Those newer to the trade might miss the true marks of moral bankruptcy because of the charm and wit and apparent normality of their client. When the victims start stacking up, or when one of them escapes to "tell all," that is when the curtain parts and the truth revealed.

Years past, the man and I had lived in the same wing. We had played as partners in card games. He was in his early twenties. I found him handsome, entertaining, charismatic, warm, cordial, humorous and sensitive. At the time, I did not know his crime and never asked.

Unless offered freely, you do not ask a man's past offences. You take him at face value. You trust your instincts about him if you mean to do business with him. As I said, I had no business with him. He was just an acquaintance.

When the door clicked open, I found my new cellie sitting, I assumed, cross-legged on the bottom bunk with a blanket covering him up to his neck. The up and down movement of his hand near his genital area would have been obvious to anyone blessed with even poor sight.

As I entered, he did not 'skip a beat' and greeted me cordially but continued to masturbate. Neither pornography nor photographs of nudity are allowed at FCC. I immediately glanced at my cellie's television. He was watching a well-known children's program on the public television channel.

Placing my TV on the desk beside his, I emptied my belongings rolled up in a blanket onto my bed and began to fill my footlocker under the small window. It was then I noticed that beside him on the bed, unseen from the door portal, were wallet-size photos of four boys eight to ten years old, their school pictures. They were a few of his six to twenty victims.

My cellie later admitted that he got the photos sent in from a partner on the outside. He claimed that they were his cousins, family. Had he not chosen to do all his time and had he participated in the year-long MOSOP group therapy, he would not have been allowed to receive or possess photos of children- family or not.

Since he 'opted out' of therapy, he, like many of the most dangerous predators, was released after he served his fourteen-year sentence and was not required, as were MOSOP graduates, to participate in therapy on the outside. In other words, because he walked down all his time, upon his release from prison, he was not placed on parole and was not required, as other sex offenders, to participate in court-ordered therapy while on parole.

Right now, the reader is thinking, 'Did I just read what I just read?' It was, at least at that time, another peculiarity of Missouri Law. COMPLETE MOSOP earn early parole date. ON PAROLE, must attend court-ordered outpatient group therapy.

OPT TO DO ALL YOUR TIME AND NOT TAKE MOSOP, get out on release date, no court-ordered therapy, no parole officer or therapist to give weekly accounts to of your whereabouts or behavior. Of course, the OPT-OUTs still had to report every three months at their jurisdiction's police station to register as sex offenders- that is, if their offenses were committed after the 1997 registration law. Enough said about that.

A few words about my understanding of and feelings about pedophilia, the sexual predator, and the treatment of predators: Emotionally, I have never understood the attraction of an adult to a prepubescent child. How can an adult be attracted sexually to a nonsexual, innocent child? It is hard to comprehend until you understand the nature of the prepubescent (or the immature or retarded pubescent), the nature of the predator, and the nature of power. It is an unholy combination.

A child is innocent and is treated so in our society. Because of their innocence, they naturally trust caregiving adults. As they grow older, the number of caregiving adults increase. It expands from mother and father to grandparents to aunts and uncles, to neighbors, babysitters, kindergarten teachers, teacher's aides, coaches, elementary school teachers, bus drivers, doctors, nurses- the list increases as the child ages. So does their level and circle of trust.

Children are trained from their earliest years to trust and depend on caregivers. They must for virtually everything. They early-on learn to obey and trust the authority figures placed over them. They have no say about it. They assume that these powerful figures are benevolent and kind, and rightly so.

Predators use their charm, lies, associations, sometimes position of authority, to groom a child into trusting them. It is not that they see the child as a sexual creature, per se. They see them as easily malleable, easily manipulated, easily controlled. Much like a serial rapist rapes out of a sense of power, so does the sexual predator of children rape to fulfill his *need* to feel powerful, in control.

In prison, I witnessed this all the time. The psychopaths, the predators did whatever it took to exercise and demonstrate their power over other inmates. However, in prison, without the natural, legal, and social constraints, the predator does not need to spend his time honing his grooming skills. He does not need to be charming, personable, or witty to groom his victims. He has almost full-reign to exercise his power over the weak. I conclude that all sex offenders and all predators are not alike. Let me explain the distinction I see.

The sex offender, who is *not* a predator, does not seek power or control. He or she seeks emotional and sexual fulfillment and may not be able to distinguish between the two. He or she has boundary issues- the difference in age or life-experience does not seem to matter. This type of sex offender may emotionally see themselves as the same age of their victim, and they emotionally may well be.

Perhaps the man has failed in his attempts at romantic relationships with adults. Perhaps he has taken on the 'safe' role of teacher, mentor, coach, or surrogate parent with a naïve young boy, girl, or teenager in the hope that a romantic relationship will develop. This takes time and a lot of grooming.

It is often hard for normal folk or even mental health professionals to observe grooming behaviors and see what is in a man's heart. We naturally want to think the best and give benefit of the doubt. After all, *we* are raised to trust in caregivers.

Another example of a sex offender who is not a predator would be a soccer mom rejected by the 'star' athlete in her school days. After a harmless and flirtatious encounter with her fourteen-year-old son's soccer mate, she texts him that she is in love with him and wants to be his *first.* These type sex offenders have a conscience, know what they are doing is wrong, and once arrested and/or in therapy admit the wrong, are truly sorry, desire and seek help to stop or control their aberrant behaviors, and want to make restitution and return to a normal life.

The difference between the sex offender seeking emotional/sexual fulfillment with a child and the true predator is that they feel *powerless*. However, in the present prosecutorial environment, there is no distinction made between them and violent predators that crave and use sex to feel *powerful.*

Although the outcome of a sex offense is violent, especially when committed on a child, the *intent* and actions of the emotional-need-fulfilling sex offender may not be. In other words, there is no physical damage done to the child. The violence, unintended, is more likely to be long-lasting psychological emotional damage. In the case of consensual sex between an adult and a teenager, there may be little to no psychological or emotional damage caused. Yet, this is not taken into consideration by judge, jury, or attorneys.

Labeled violent and imprisoned, the emotional-need-fulfillers must take the MOSOP. They sit through therapy sessions beside true predators with which they have nothing in common. Treated as monsters, they feel even more hopeless and powerless to change for the better.

My cellie would appear harmless. As I have shown, he was a grooming predator- the second most dangerous type of sex offender. This came naturally to him after he conditioned himself or was conditioned by his abuser to get what he wanted from children through grooming behaviors. He was not after power on the yard, or even over himself- he cared nothing about self-control. He wanted power, control over the innocent.

Twenty-four hours a day, this was the man's fantasy. This was his focus. This was his passion- to "pop a boy's cherry," as he bluntly put it- to be his "first."

Oddly, most male sex offenders will not admit to having been sexually abused as children. Nevertheless, I think most were. They don't admit it maybe because of pride, ego; but I think it is mostly to protect their abuser- a close and loved family member, friend, or neighbor.

Simply stated, regardless of their once-relationship with their emotional/sexual need-fulfilling abuser, the child victim, like many adult victims, remembers and focuses on the normal acts of kindness and love shown to them. They believe in their hearts that their abuser loved them and never meant them any harm.

Let me be clear on this: *Power, domination and control, has nothing to do with love whether the controller is claiming to love a child or an adult.* Love uses power and authority for the welfare and good of the one loved. True power, legitimate power, protects.

My cellie and several other grooming pedophile predators, whom I met at FCC, who targeted boys, could not separate familial, platonic, or any other type of love from sex. Emotional *need* does not factor into the equation when talking about true predators. Their motivation is *greed*.

Predators covet and want to control prepubescent children. They want to use them for their sexual gratification. The only rewards gained are momentary relief from lust-driven thoughts and desires and a feeling of power, of feeling in control of their victim.

The victims of grooming predators are *nearby*- family, neighbors, kids in their care. It is hard for sex offenders to see their actions as unnatural and as rape- as harmful, especially when there is no penetration. However, the most dangerous pedophile predators are not the groomers.

The most dangerous pedophile predators are the cruising 'grab-n-run' predators. They are opportunists, dangerous, violent, unpredictable *hunters* and not just men who avail themselves of children within their easy sphere of influence. These *hunters* are the most likely to torture and murder their victims, male or female.

The heterosexual sex offenders I spoke to who had molested girls, even baby girls, did not speak of their actions as love. They referred to them in terms as if they were describing a fetish, as if girls were not persons with feelings. To them, it was as if they were using a plastic woman or a Fleshlight to get off. The abusers of prepubescent girls, or baby girls, had complete emotional detachment and sought to commit sexual violence upon them.

However, they willingly and coldly acknowledged- with almost bitter prejudice at the idea- that their actions were unnatural, violent rape. The grooming predators of boys, almost to a man, would rarely acknowledge their actions as unnatural or violent. After all, they were only doing what was done to them when they were prepubescent or pubescent.

Although these disclosures and my 'reality' sickened me, I must confess that most of my discomfort in living with my cellie was from living with him, not from his disturbing predatory pathology. I could place myself in the gym or in the library during morning 'movement' when children's programming was on television.

It was not just a once-in-a-while jerk-off under a blanket. I can understand that, even in the middle of the day. A man needs 'release' once-in-a-while.

My last cellie masturbated continually with photos of his "cousins" nearby- even after lights out. When he thought I was reading or watching my TV (with headphones on, of course), he would drop the blanket and whack away. It was an endless pleasuring or 'edging' without a fulfilling consummation.

Do not get me wrong, I was grateful that he was in no way attracted to me. I could take a piss or a dump and he would never glance at me. At times, knowing that he was turned-on by prepubescent boys caused me to feel sick and angry. Knowing that he was going to walk out of prison one day without any therapy inside or out made my blood boil; and yes, I more than once encouraged him to get help. (More about sex offender laws later.)

I was not mad at my cellie. I had the deepest sympathy for him. "There, but for the grace of God, go

I." I do not know what horrors were done to him when a child to make him so.

Upon reflection, I believe there was no horror in his molesting at all. His molester must have been the gentlest- the tenderest and most trusting of groomers. I was mad as hell at the state.

Missouri has an answer for the irredeemable, unsalvageable predators. Aptly enough, it is labeled, *The Predator Unit.* It is a lockdown mental health facility located on the FCC prison grounds. Men and women who have multiple victims are sometimes placed there, though they may have completed their sentences and the MOSOP. Once a year, the "patients" may appeal to therapists and a judge to review their case and "progress" to be considered for release. However, they may be left there for the duration of their lives.

At this writing, there are 179 people residing in The Predator Unit with twenty-six waiting in county jails or mental health facilities to be admitted. In eleven years only two have been released and that against the recommendation of the on-site therapists.

I have often wondered if my last cellie and the other men I thought to be true predators ended up in The Predator Unit. I have also wondered how many non-predatory sex offenders, perhaps misdiagnosed, trapped there with little hope of getting out.

Truly, Dante's *"Gates of Hell"* greeting hangs just above the door.

Gabriel's Story

You learn a lot about a man by talking with his mother. That privilege, as you can imagine, is rare in prison. Shared letters from moms can accomplish the same thing. The tone in her written words speaks volumes. No love is greater except maybe God's love.

No matter how devout a believer he is, a mother's love is more tangible to a man. Maybe that is why, whether on the battlefield or in the field hospital, the young dying soldier's last thoughts and breathe go to his mother. She is always ever-present, even at death, even if she has passed on before you.

The love a son has for his mother also speaks volumes. The thing that defined Gabriel, which I was the first to discover after his longtime lover, was *not* that he was a convict, prostitute, pimp or thug. He saw himself, defined himself by his mother's love and by his for his mother- that, and his Greek heritage. In the quiet recesses of his cell and soul, it was who Gabriel truly was- who he was in his core. (It is impossible I think for purebloods to think of their mothers without thinking of their heritage or visa-versa.)

The reader knows what I am talking about. You have seen countless examples of a mother's power and influence over her son; probably so many that you now do not take the time to notice them. A big gorilla of a man who can smash you down to atoms is brought to heel by one disapproving glance from his mother. No matter how old the man, he is still "my little boy."

At our first meeting, Gabriel told me, "I haven't always been like this." It was his way of saying he was sorry for what he had become despite his mother's nurturing, love, and prayers. Disappointing her was his greatest regret. It is the hardest thing in the world for a man to bear- the knowledge that he has sinned against mother's love.

The next hardest thing is to cause mother pain- to cause her to suffer. But that is what we 'sons of Adam' do. From kicks in the womb, to the labor pains of birth and delivery, to fights with our old man, we cause mom pain. It may be the root of most of a man's guilt, because failing mom is really failing yourself and your father.

It was at the yard's confessional, the bleachers, where Gabriel eventually trusted me enough to bare his soul, to share his story. I did not solicit it or even expect it. When it did come, I bowed in humility to a true Word Weaver. His words were plain, but his heart was elegant, enlightened, and mirrored the beauty of his outer self.

Most of the time we expect that a man's words will mirror his outer self, that they will be an expression of his experiences, his job, his friendships and loves. Listening to a man who had been incarcerated from the age of sixteen, who had his manhood all but driven out of him, who had been crushed so many times that his only out was to beef-up and become a crusher, I expected and did hear a sad soul-crushing tale.

However, flowing in Gabriel's river of words, filled with swirling whirlpools, long dropping spillways, and turbulent terrifying rapids, I heard a trickle of hope. Though you, until now, may have seen him as a monster, I surely saw him as one at the first, join me and hear the story of the man. Join me at the river's edge and listen. Hear Gabriel speak his own story.

"My grandparents, my father's people emigrated here from Greece. They worked hard- pappoos worked at a vinegar barrel factory, yiayia worked at an industrial laundry and took in sewing. My parents were born in St. Louis. That's where my grandparents settled. I was born there, too.

"Pappoos eventually bought a two-story house near the downtown that had been used as a boarding house. My grandparents lived on the top floor with my two aunts until they married. When my father married, he and mama lived on the first floor with his two brothers sharing a bedroom in the back. It was quite crowed at times.

"Eventually, pappoos and yiayia started a business and were able to buy a bigger house in Clayton. My parents worked for them and eventually took ownership of the business. So, you see, I wasn't raised on the wrong side of the tracks, Old-g. I was born with a silver spoon in my mouth. I guess I swallowed it."

Gabriel paused, looked around the yard- watching his back- cracked a reassuring smile, and jumped off the bleachers onto the ground. With arms spread wide, he walked around.

"This is not me.

"You want to know me, who I really am?

"I am Greek!"

Any inmate on the yard who witnessed that display did not see or hear it. Gabriel was the kind of man whose cell extended to the yard and beyond. They bowed their heads or looked away, tucked their tails and kept walking. For just a moment, I thought I was going to see him do a 'Greek' dance. You know, like the ones you see at their weddings. He continued.

"Most of you 'English' don't know anything about us, except maybe for our Baklava or our Shish Kabobs. You've probably never eaten lamb, and you surely won't get any Greek cuisine in this shit hole." (I had, with mint sauce, and in Euros, and I do love Baklava and Shish Kabobs.)

"We gave you democracy. We gave you philosophy. We gave you the architecture that adorns your buildings. Those are our Doric and Corinthian and Ionic columns, our porticos, our statues and our reliefs on your government buildings and banks."

Gabriel looked around again and calming himself, took a seat near me. He exhaled hard.

"Why did that 'Roman' have to make me a slave? Why did he send me here?"

An avid history buff, I immediately understood Gabriel's meaning. The Romans had conquered the Greeks, as they did everyone else in the Mediterranean, enslaved them, and incorporated their language, art, and culture into their own. Gabriel was verbally asking why the judge had done this to him. Internally, he was asking the question all incarcerated men ask themselves daily, "Why did I do this to myself?"

Putting aside his prison-conditioned conscience, Gabriel continued, "I was born with a silver spoon in my mouth. One mistake...one horrible mistake destroyed me. I will never be *me* again. Even if I get to leave this place, I will never be me again.

"Do you have a problem with my heritage?"

"No, I agree with all that you've said. But why is it so important to you in this place at this time?"

"Because Old-g, it's all that's left of me."

Tears brimmed in Gabriel's eyes as he scooted forward and grabbed my shirt with both hands.

"It's not just who I am; it's all that's left of me.

"I know what you're thinking. You're thinking that my people's past is just a shadow- meaningless in this day, in this place. But you are wrong. A shadow is but a dark reflection of a reality."

Gabriel paused again, composed himself, and scooted back a few feet. He relaxed and stretched his arms wide along the bleacher board behind him.

"You tell anybody this, and I will kick your ass around this yard until hades takes you."

Gabriel studied me then winked and smiled, as if he was amused about what he was going to disclose.

"My middle name is Alexandros, Alexander. Only my lover knows that.

"When I turned eighteen, I wasn't given a birthday party. I was taken from the Juvenile Center to The Walls- that dark hole of a Civil War prison. I was bought as soon as my feet hit the ground.

"It's not like here. There, are so many dark godless guardless places. At times, I felt like I was in Plato's cave.

"You've heard that you can't rape the willing? But you can rape a man until he *is* willing. Although I was small and weak, I fought back. No one can win against a gangbang.

"It was at The Walls that I learned my trade and the business. I studied the pimps, the pushers, and the players. Then I transferred to Boonville, then to Cross Roads.

"On the bus ride to Boonville, I determined to enter Gabriel but to leave that place Alexander. I worked out four hours a day, jogged, and the rest of the time made my mind strong. I got my G.E.D. and worked in the library and read a lot."

Gabriel paused to study me again. I decided to ask the question pressing my mind.

"Gabriel, may I ask a question about what you just said?"

He nodded.

"What do you mean? Why did you have to go into Boonville as Gabriel but come out as Alexander? You still go by Gabriel."

"You think I wanted to know myself perhaps after the name of a Greek Orthodox Patriarch? Hell, no. I determined to come out of there as the greatest of all Greeks who had the good fortune of being born in the Kingdom of Macedon.

"I determined to come out of Boonville strong, a leader, on top. I determined to come out of there as the greatest Greek of all time, Alexander the Great."

"The yard is closed, the yard is closed. Return to your houses for count time."

"Tomorrow, I'll talk about my mama and about my lover- same time same place. Don't be late."

I nodded my 'ok' and headed for my house wondering if Gabriel was delusional, or if I was missing something. The revelations of the next day would put my mind to rest then disturb it all over again.

Day two of the confession:

"I will only say this about my crime. Drunk, high, and stupid, a few friends and I committed armed criminal action. That is all you need to know.

"My crime and conviction did devastate my mother and father. Dad died a few years later, and I attended the graveside ceremony in shackles under guard. As mama continually looked at me, I wondered if her tears were more for me. ...If I only had a chance to do it all over again..."

Gabriel stood up and pulled off his T-shirt in one motion. Knowing the reality of the yard, and whom I was with, I immediately looked around for a threat. Men only pull off their shirts like that because they are getting ready for a fight. He continued his confession.

"All you really have is your family. That's your reality. Several months before my incarceration, while my case appealed, I paid an amazing tattoo artist to make my back his Sistine Chapel. I gave him a photo of my mother holding me as a baby. The tattoo, which men rarely see, is of the Madonna and child."

Gabriel turned around revealing a tattoo from the top of his back to his waistline. It was the most detailed and beautiful tattoo I have, to this day, ever seen. It was a masterpiece just like Michelangelo's Sistine Chapel in Rome. However, it reminded me more of a painting by Raphael. Gabriel put on his shirt and sat back down.

"Two things I didn't think about during those weeks of tattooing.

"One: with the polished stainless steel mirrors they give us in here, I could never really see and appreciate it.

Luckily, during one of my visits with mama, I got the photographer to take a picture of it for me.

"Two: I couldn't have known that all those men who would fuck me in the future would see it.

"At first, I thought, 'yeah, have a little guilt with your fuck boys. Mama's looking at what you're doing to her son,' but I could not do that to mama.

"Ask any of my clients, not one man has every fucked me with my shirt off- at least doggie-style. If I'm on my back and they want the full treatment, then I take my shirt off. But no one sees mama, except for my lover, and now you."

"You haven't spoken much about your lover. What's his real name?" It seemed to me an appropriate time to find out the real name of the man whose letters I had been reading.

"Hephaiston; he was and always shall be the lover of Alexander."

'Here we go again,' I thought.

"That's what the 'H' initial of his name means, Hephaiston?" I begged for clarification. The letters were always signed, 'H'.

"Old-g, if you breathe a word of any of this, I swear to God, I will sell your white ass to the lowest black-gangsta bidder.

"My lover's name is Herbert. Who names their kid 'Herbert' these days? I call him Herbie. We met not long after he arrived here several years ago. He volunteered to spot me on the bench. It was love at first sight.

"Shortly after that I arranged for Herbie to be moved to my cell. We eventually moved to more premium real estate- a larger corner cell with a view of the yard. The various caseworkers over the years allowed us to be cellies. I'm the lead janitor in six-house, you know. It affords some privileges.

"Both of us were long-timers, so there was no impropriety in the request. You've probably noticed the few old fag couples in here that have shared the same cell for years."

I acknowledged that I knew of them.

"Gabriel, may I ask a few more questions about you and Herbie?"

"Shoot."

"You got the tattoo of your mother on your back because you love her probably more than anyone or anything. Do you have a tattoo of Herbie, too?"

"Well, I was going to have his name tattooed on my dick. But I have the name of the girl I lost my virginity to there, and it didn't seem appropriate. Her name is Missi, spelled 'M-I-S-S-I,' and we lost our virginity to each other at sixteen."

"That's an odd spelling. Isn't it supposed to end with a 'y'?"

"Well yeah, but that's only what it spells when my dick is soft. When it's hard it spells the name of a state."

"Missouri?"

"Mississippi."

"Why Mississippi," I asked.

At the question, Gabriel had a hearty laugh. He leaned forward and addressed me again.

"Because fish, it shows how long my Greek prick is." Gabriel laughed heartily again. I did not. I was, I confess, confused.

"Old-g, it is the oldest dick joke in the world. I'm just fucking with you. My first and last girlfriend's name was Diane. Herbie's name is the only name I have tattooed on my pecker.

"And as a heads-up, if you decide to have something tattooed on your penis, wait until you are out of here. It hurts so bad that you really need to be well-drunk when you do it."

"Wow, you must really love the guy to get his name put on your dick in here."

"Don't fret over it. We held hands and used toothache medicine to numb it some. Besides, he almost got the worst end of that deal. He still thanks the stars that he had too small a cock for it."

I registered confusion. Gabriel explained.

"At first, I insisted that he tat the name *Alexander's* or better, *Alexander the Great's* on his. But then, I would've had to get *Hephaiston's* tatted on mine. *Herbie's* is a lot shorter and has near the same amount of letters as *Gabriel's*. Hell, halfway through it, I almost settled for just *Herb's*."

Gabriel laughed a little but then went silent, looked down then up at me again. Something in his gray grave demeanor signaled that he was about to reveal the real reason he was telling his story, that he was about to tell the actual story he wanted me to know. I confess it was quite a shock to hear it.

"A year after Herbie and I shacked up, I was diagnosed to have H.I.V. I had practiced safe sex...at least as safe as you can without a condom. I wouldn't let guys cum in me. But I think I must've got it at The Walls at the first."

Gabriel went silent again, looked away then down.

"Honestly, I stopped fucking around when I found out. I only participate in the business end now, except for the occasional blowjob, if required.

"I have no idea how many men I infected..."

Gabriel's eyes watered and he wiped his flowing tears with his shirt. I anticipated what came next.

"Knowing the risk, that I might have it, I was extra careful with Herbie. I dry-humped him, but never came in him. We did a lot of sixty-nining.

"We shed a lot of tears over it and had more than a few fights about it. I tried to push him away, but he refused to go. I denied him sex for weeks. The more I pushed the harder he clung to me.

"One night, I woke up to him sucking me. Once I was fully erect and alert, he looked into my eyes then dropped down and assumed the position. I knew what he wanted. If his Alexander was going to die, he wanted to die with him.

"It wasn't sex that time. It was love. I did it. I released in him. After that, we made love without fear or restraint. Then a few months ago, he was released, got his walking papers, and I will never take another lover.

"As you read in his letters, it's a different world out there now. To be honest, I'm afraid to go back into it. Technology has changed everything.

"Thirteen years I've been on the inside- well, fifteen in total. If I develop full-blown A.I.D.S., I may not make it out of here. If I do develop A.I.D.S., they'll probably release me early. They don't want to pay the bills from that."

I did not dare interrupt at this point. I thought it best to let Gabriel finish- to reveal his final close-guarded cards.

"Herbie is living with my mama and yiayia. His father would not allow him to come home since he is gay. Mama loves him like a son- like she loves me. Maybe I will get early release because of this disease. Maybe Alexandros and Hephaiston will be together until the end.

"Old-g, we're in the real world now. I want to ask a few favors."

"Anything, name it," I answered tearfully.

"I want you to tell our story one day- me and Hephaiston's. Maybe it will keep some snot-nosed Greek boy from ending up in a place like this."

"To be honest Alexander, I don't see myself thinking about, much less writing about this place. I want to forget it."

"You may for a while, but it will all come back. When it does, tell my story as I would have you tell it. Promise me that."

"I promise I will, Gabriel Alexandros."

"The final favor...we can never meet again. These talks have put a target on your back. It's not safe for you. Even Old-G is asking, "what the hell," is between us. Conspiracy theories abound." He grinned, said, "Right-on," and walked away without looking back.

"Thank you, Gabriel."

(Gabriel and Herbie's love story is in part two entitled, Alexander and Hephaiston.)

The Jester

It was the most horrific of human screams. It tore through the cold concrete steel walls of our prison home leaving them paper-thin with our suddenly rattled nerves. Like a protesting poltergeist leaving its guilt-stained bloodied blots upon cells and souls, the warm-blooded man-boy cried out in absolute anguish, causing our corporate blood to run cold.

It was not a cry for vendetta or revenge- the cry of 'the most of us' who have been unspeakably unrightably wronged. It was the eternally haunting asked, "Why?" that we heard from the cell so far, yet so near to our own.

Several of us who had befriended him, warned him. Time and time again we warned him. We went out of our way to walk with him, to talk with him, to protect him. Nevertheless, like bees to honey, the ghetto gangstas were drawn to him. Leaving him unattended one minute, one second in the chow line or library or gym or at school, they were there whispering in his ear. Whispers that made him laugh, that in turn made them laugh. Theirs was a sadistic laugh.

How they lured him to the secret place, the dark closet, that mid-afternoon, we never knew. It was in a building basement where 'honor' inmates worked- no CO was present for more than a few minutes every few hours. It was a place reserved for 'a couple' to 'motel-in' for thirty minutes; they dare not linger longer. Four men entered with the Jester.

It is impossible to scream for help with a doubled-sock balled in your mouth. It was not a sock that prevented the man-boy's screams that day. Two pair of muscular arms held him as one man raped one end of him and the other raped the other end. Then they switched-up and the unspeakable violations began again.

Terror itself witnessed what happened in that dark place amidst the four dark figures and wept for the death of innocence.

How much, for a room with no view? What 'honor' inmate was so beyond the reach of conscience that he opened the door and let the four in with the man-boy, took his payment and shut it behind? Surely, he heard through paper-thin wooden door and his paper-thin heart what they heard in that dark place. Surely, they heard through muffled protest what we heard an hour later when the man-boy somehow managed to return obediently to his cell for the count. Did it haunt them as it haunted us? No.

"What could have prevented the rape," you ask? Twenty dollars per week to 'buy' protection, is the answer- that, from a man who made seven dollars a month from his state stipend. You protest, "How could he afford that?" How could he and many like him not afford to pay?

To understand what happened that day, you must understand the man, and understand what the man did not and could not understand until that day. The Jester, twenty at the time, was incarcerated for exposing himself to an eight-year-old neighbor girl, and for having her expose herself to him. "I'll show you mine, if you show me yours." It never went beyond that.

This man-boy was born with umbilical cord wrapped around his neck, depriving his brain of oxygen for some time. His mother died in childbirth. The baby boy lived but suffered from diminished mental capacity. He spent his life in special education classes in the small town where his father raised him alone. When he "graduated" high school, he became a very lonely young man.

Although the man-boy did not penetrate the little girl's vagina, he obviously was curious about female anatomy and wanted to see it. Although psychiatrists and former teachers and caregivers testified that he saw himself not as a man, but as the same age as the little girl and was playing doctor, the prosecuting attorney representing the sovereign interests of the state made sure this young man was sentenced to five years and ordered to complete the MOSOP.

In my conversations with the Jester, asking him if he understood that his exposing himself to the little girl was morally wrong and illegal, each time he admitted, "Yes." It became clear to me that he really did not understand. He really did not care why he was in prison. There he found new friends to replace the ones he had lost from high school. Every man was his friend.

The Jester daily attended G.E.D. classes, but did not understand the difference between a subject and a predicate. He never mastered more than simple multiplication and division. He did learn how to write a check, but could rarely balance his checkbook. It was all a game to him- a wonderful game with his new friends. He laughed at his failures and more at his successes.

One of the Jester's greatest entertainments was listening to me read my made-up love stories. He was such a genuine honest soul and a captive audience. If he laughed and cried in the 'right' spots, I knew the story was right. Eventually, he asked me to write a love story with him in it. His only conditions: that he be funny, look funny, be the hero, and win the girl. It was a great challenge.

In preparation, as I did with all the men for whom I wrote, I asked the Jester his favorite stories- books, films, comic books. He replied, *"The Three Musketeers,* and *The Hunchback from Notre Dame,"* two of my favorites from the pens of the great French authors Alexander Dumas and Victor Hugo. That made the work much more interesting. (The reader will find that story in part two entitled, Esmeralda and Quasimodo, the Hunchback Telemarketeer: A Fairy Tale.)

Did the man-boy pass the MOSOP? No. Like many of the functionally illiterate, how could he understand the therapeutic concepts, memorize fifteen or so lengthy principles word and punctuation perfect, other equally wordy criteria using such words as 'homeostasis' and write them weekly on a test for a year? How could he understand that the state, society, saw him and required him to see himself as a monster? Maybe that is why he wanted to see himself as Quasimodo.

How did the Jester daily respond to hearing men describe in group therapy how they had groomed, abused and molested their victims? He laughed. He laughed everywhere, at everything, all the time. It was all funny to him. Rebuked and reprimanded by the therapist and fellow group members, he would go quiet and blush.

When the gangstas whispered in his ear what he was going to 'give up' to them, the Jester laughed and repeated their threats. If you visited his cell during open wing, or if you stood with him in chow line, he would say loudly, "I'm going to suck your dick! Pull it out and I'll suck it right now. I want you to fuck me. I want you to fuck me hard in the ass." They pinched his butt, so he pinched ours. To him it was all wonderful play. He was loved, accepted.

Laughing, the Jester would ignore our immediate hushes, rebukes, and warnings. He could not grasp that a man would suck another man's dick. His daddy had told him that only queers did that, and would follow the remark with, "You know steers and queers come from Texas." There were no queers at FCC except for the guys who dressed like girls. And what man would let another man fuck him in the ass? He could not grasp the concept of a *mangina*.

"Men don't have a pussy," he would remark, then laugh heartily, "and I've seen me a pussy." As I said, he laughed all the time at everything. It was all a game- even threats whispered in the ear.

For a year, I had been reading the Jester's letters from his father and writing response letters for him. Twice a week I would sit down with the man-boy, read a few lines of his father's letters, ask for a response and pen it. They, of course, were not love letters, but they were loving letters. This young man loved his father very much. After all, the man had been both mother and father to the boy and had bent over backwards to accommodate his every need.

After the gang rape, in the solitude of his cell, the man-boy did not cry for his father. The violation upon his person was so beyond his limited capacity to understand that I am sure he felt his father would not understand it. Therefore, instead of crying out for his father, or for God as an extension of his father, he screamed out repeatedly the eternally haunting, "Why?"

Thankfully, this occurred when the night COs were on duty. The daytime COs seemed callous and indifferent or sometimes downright hostile to the inmates, treating us as if we were walking piles of excrement. CO 'C' was not that way. Although he did not take shit off anyone, he treated each man as a man with respect.

'C' was on duty walking from cell to cell counting when the Jester screamed out in pain and cried alone in his cell. 'C' paused and asked what the matter was, told the man-boy to try to get control of his self, and continued count. When the locks popped to let us out for evening chow, 'C' again tried to find out what was causing the weeping, rocking, and moaning. The Jester closed his door and returned to his bunk weeping.

After chow time, when open wing was called, several of us immediately went to the Jester's cell. 'C' arrived shortly after and stood witness as we each tried to comfort and reassure, as we tried to find out what happened that had so upset the young man. He would not say anything but "Why?" repeatedly, rocking and weeping, holding a gray wool blanket.

The Jester was not himself after that. He did not laugh. He did not joke. He did not jokingly invite anyone to fuck him in the ass. It was days before he finally told me what had happened and pointed out the men who had done it.

The reader probably assumes that I immediately told the powers-that-be. However, I did not have a death wish or a wish to be transferred to another camp, or to

ADSEG. Some inmates talk to COs. What happens in the cell stays in the cell, but not if a CO gets involved.

The reader might think that I went to Henry or to Gabriel with the problem. Again, this I did not do. It was inappropriate on several levels, violating many aspects of prison etiquette and protocol. You do not try to pit one pimp or gang leader against another. It probably would have ignited a race riot. Skin color was not the issue. It was the violation and making sure it did not happen again.

My only recourse was to contact my old cellie, Earl. His prison job gave him access to both A and B-sides of the camp. As I stated before, he seemed in good standing with the COs and caseworkers- he always seemed to get what he wanted from them. We met on the bleachers and I told him what had happened to the Jester.

Earl was immediately red-faced and livid. He too felt protective and fond of the man-boy. I told him the names of the gangstas and their demand for twenty dollars per week for protection. When the man-boy met Earl later on and confirmed his story, he assured Earl that he was all right, and that his daddy was coming to the prison to kill those men. (This was the Jester's fantasy- the humiliation talking- and not the result of any communication that he had with his father. His father never knew of the rape.)

As most men of unseen influence in prison, Earl spoke to 'whomever'; they spoke to 'whomever', and the contract on the man-boy was dropped as was the demand for protection money. By the time Earl's contacts had finished with the gangstas who had raped the Jester, their only conditional demand to leave the "retard" alone was that he never admit the rape and never acknowledge them as the rapists. This, the Jester gladly agreed to and soon after recovered his sense of humor, but minus the sexual jokes and innuendo.

Soon after the intervention, I was transferred to the other side of the camp and remained there three or so months before transferring back. (For all I know, this was arranged to get me out of the way for a while- for my protection.) Other tutors assisted the Jester in writing letters to his father. Eventually, he was moved and assigned a cellie who gladly took on the privilege. (None of us ever asked for or received a dime for helping this young man with the reading or writing of letters, for being his friends, or for the genuine protection mysteriously made available to him.)

I can report to the reader that the 'honor' inmate who facilitated the rape was shipped out shortly thereafter. The inmates who raped the Jester were shipped out, too. Who knows what awaited them at their new prison homes? Consequences for crimes like theirs, even in prison, follow you. Justice served.

What was said to higher authorities to protect our friend can easily be surmised. What was done to protect the man-boy, and who did the protecting on the inside is not so easy to determine. Earl was a *player* not a protector, not a powerbroker on the yard. He was instrumental in arranging protection for the man-boy, and for that, I was and am to this day grateful. Many other vulnerable and naïve young men in the penile system are not so fortunate.

Whether it is the educational system, the welfare system, the healthcare system or the prison system, many people fall through the cracks. It is a bureaucratic truth, if nothing else. The Jester and many like him should not be placed in prison. He was not only functionally illiterate; he had the reasoning faculties and emotional makeup of a child. He was a man-boy.

The Jester, as you have already surmised, is not his name, and I did not use the humorous title he coined for himself, because those at FCC at the time would readily know him. With my description of him and of his circumstances and troubles, I am sure some may guess his identity.

Recently, I spoke to a man who has kept in contact with the Jester for all these years. He reported that he is well, working part-time, and living with his beloved father. I often wondered if he ever told him of the rape. I sincerely doubt that he did. It would not have been in his nature or in the nature of most men to do so. From the time he was a baby in his father's arms, the Jester I am sure, was a happy, cooing, smiling, giggling child. He remains so as a free man and registered sex offender.

What the Jester did in exposing himself to the little girl was wrong. However, was prison the best and only option for him? For many maybe it is, but for a person of diminished mental capacity whose every action and reaction and emotion is child-like, I believe it is the worst horror you could bring upon them. They never understand *why* they are placed there, and never have the capabilities or capacity to pass the 'state requirements' like graduating the G.E.D. program or passing the MOSOP.

Billy

Billy was as common as cucumber on a garden salad. He is the early twenty-something stock boy you find at any local discount store. He had low to no ambition other than to earn a living wage, come home, smoke a little weed, guzzle some suds, and make love to a beautiful wife on the pill- need to hold off on children for a while.

The man was of average intelligence, average wit, average height and weight, loved sports and hunting and bowling- *if* they ended in partying. He did not see that he was put here by divine plan, and if there was a God, surely he or she was merciful and would give him- a decent man who always tried to do the right thing and help a neighbor in need- a break on the Day of Judgment.

It is here that I must forewarn the reader that Billy's story is the most common and at the same time the most complex and lengthy to tell. His story involves jealousy, conspiracy, naivety, stupidity, and political events and decisions involving the highest levels of the Missouri, Texas, and Federal governments.

Billy arrived at FCC in late 1997, as I recall, on a bus *not* from Fulton or from a Missouri jail. Like hundreds of Missouri men at the time, he arrived "home" after being housed in a Texas jail for two years- emaciated. (*Cell leasing* was the name of the program.) Billy and the men, who stepped onto the FCC yard that day, were the first I had seen that did not get catcalls and threatening comments. 'Fresh' fish had *not* arrived.

A few weeks before the arrival of Billy and the hundreds of others, we all watched the drama play out on local and national television. You see, because of overcrowding, Missouri thought it expedient to pay Texas millions of dollars to house several hundreds of their inmates while new prisons were being built. What the Missouri Department of Corrections did not know and should have known, was that in the Texas jails our boys were starved and stacked like true cordwood in bunk beds so close they might as well have been sleeping with each other- ceiling lights on twenty-four hours a day. In addition, there was no 'yard time' or recreation allowed.

The video that surfaced was not meant for public consumption. It was a training video of the Texas Department of Corrections version of *Goon Squads*. German Shepherds were brought into the open bays. Missouri men in boxers, towels, or naked were ordered to lie down on the bare cold concrete floor for hours as the dogs sniffed them from head to toe and their bunks for contraband.

Someone with a conscience, or maybe for monetary gain, smuggled the video out and gave or sold it to a TV news affiliate. At that point, it went national. The emaciated state of the men was not the only thing that disturbed common folk across Missouri and the nation. Seeing those dangerous attack dogs growling, snarling, and sniffing the men from head to toe was upsetting, as well.

In one incident, a dog attacked a man who had grown weary of lying for two hours in the same position on the cold concrete stretching a little to unfreeze his joints. He moved his leg a few inches, the dog attacked. Mace or Pepper spray was also freely used on complaining but compliant men lying naked or almost naked on the freezing floors.

Individual inmates filed lawsuits followed by many joining to file Class-Action suits. Descent Missouri folk cried out, "Bring our battered boys home." The outcry did not land on a Governor's deaf ears.

Many inmates at FCC were suddenly transferred to other prisons and room was made for the return of the *Texas* men. The FCC gymnasium was 'modified' and bunk beds were installed on the basketball court. The empty bays of five-house, which housed the 'hole', were also used to house the returning men.

The reader surely remembers that in the late 1980s under the first Bush Administration and during the 1990s during the Clinton Administration, that many misdemeanors involving drunk driving, illegal drugs, and sex were reclassified as felonies- new laws written at the federal and state levels. An offense that once got you three months to a year in the local 'pokey' now got you five-to-ten in the pen. Federal grants were awarded to add one hundred thousand needed police officers to our city streets.

New prisons were built with billions in Federal Grant money. The statistics prove this. During the 1990s, the prison population in Missouri and across the nation *doubled*. By this writing, it has almost tripled.

Suddenly, rural communities in Missouri bid for new prisons within their jurisdictions. Struggling farming communities vied for the privilege of having a penitentiary built in their back yards. It was a boon to small towns across Missouri and the nation.

The reality: New prisons must be filled up so as not to lose Federal grant monies. 'Tough on Criminals' became the watchword and the clarion call. Judges handed down harsh sentences for what many considered minor or questionable offenses- especially if committed by a repeat offender.

Politically ambitious Prosecuting Attorneys put men and women away on the flimsiest of circumstantial evidence. Overcrowding at the city and county jails, at the Reception and Diagnostic Centers, and the already overcrowded prisons was the only outcome that could have come from this.

Other than 'bringing our battered boys' back from Texas, and some of them winning a few thousand dollars in compensation for their suffering, did anything really change? No. As many states mindlessly followed the California action to curb crime with their 'Three Strikes and you're out' law, many thousands of *nonviolent* men and women were and are incarcerated in Missouri and across the nation for many years at taxpayer expense. (It is my understanding that the United States now has the infamous honor of having more of its citizens incarcerated than any country on earth.)

Under the new laws, most first-time nonviolent, now *labeled-violent* offenders face certain incarceration. In the 1980s and before, nonviolent offenders were ordered to do community service and or to complete court-ordered therapy. Now, they sit in cells. Before the 1990's changes, most of these offenders would have remained in their communities working, earning a wage, paying taxes, raising their children while under some kind of probation or supervision, not wasting away for years in cells at taxpayer expense.

The cost of inmate room and board is only a fraction of the expenses incurred. Health care for the increasing jail and prison populations must be provided. The states also must come up with the resources to pay for the court-ordered sexual and substance abuse programs- the therapists and staffs needed.

Then there is the creation of a new underclass of repeat offenders to consider. This requires the hiring of many new COs and parole officers, caseworkers and staff. More teachers for prison G.E.D. schools also are required. The rising expenses go on and on to this day with no end in sight.

Denied their breadwinners, families are added to the welfare and food stamp rolls. On both sides of the razor wire fence, we find hundreds of thousands of lives ruined. Petty offenders evolve into hardened criminal repeat offenders.

In the case of sex crimes, there is no distinction made between men like 'the Jester' and others with mental disorders or emotional problems and the predators. There is no distinction made in sexual offences. *Therapy is a punitive process meant to, if you will, separate the wheat from the chaff- the non-predatory from the predatory sex offender. This is not therapy.*

The hundreds of thousands of family members of the men and women incarcerated then and now know what I am talking about. They lived through it and still suffer from the intended and unintended consequences of these new 'tough on criminals' legal standards and policies. They have become the newly disenfranchised.

A note of clarification: If a psychiatric evaluation finds that a person is nonviolent, not a threat, and that he or she will be harmed and not rehabilitated in prison, why put him or her there? I am not saying that there are not hundreds of thousands of psychopathic personalities who need to be incarcerated- violent, conscienceless men and women who have indeed horribly harmed and created victims, and who need to be removed from society. They do and are. However, this country has millions of men and women incarcerated long-term, many because they committed more than a few petty crimes.

States and communities have long heard the 'bark' and now are feeling the 'bite' of this untenable situation. Governors are and will soon be releasing thousands of inmates early because their states are in financial crisis partly from this expense. I've recently observed that some states still holding to the 'tough on criminals' stance, are foolishly laying off thousands of teachers, firefighters, law enforcement officers, social workers, doctors and nurses instead of releasing nonviolent 'labeled-violent' offenders. It will be a cold day in hell before those states release these 'violent' offenders from their sinking ships of state onto the streets.

Early release for most is not a favor. Have you ever tried to find a job with a felony and prison time on your record...not to mention if you are a labeled sex offender? (At this writing, of those on sex offender registration lists, 56% are unemployed in Missouri. Of the 44% employed, many are underemployed. I wonder what the suicide statistics is for this group.)

Unless the paroled-offender has a relative or friend who owns a business...good luck with that early release thing you got going for you. The 'ex-felon' finds that he or she is part of the newly disenfranchised and will desperately accept a part-time job with no benefits that pays minimum wage and bitterly mourn the death of 'The American Dream'. In other words: *If you commit a non-violent crime in this country, like a debt incurred in prison that can never be fully repaid, you will continue paying for that crime the rest of your life!*

Billy represents the many 'labeled' and convicted sex offenders that refused the MOSOP. They walked down all their time and spent countless hours in the law room of the prison library researching and writing endless appeals protesting their innocence. To somewhat understand Billy's peculiar situation, the reader must understand that, at that time at least, a convicted sex offender had to agree with his alleged victim's account of what happened between them in order to be put on the almost two-year waiting list to enter the Missouri Sexual-Offender Program.

As I have shown before, many men whom I deemed to be true predators refused the MOSOP and walked down their time, and upon release were not required to be on parole or to continue in group therapy. However, some men refused the MOSOP protesting their innocence. I am further convinced that many lied, agreed with their accusers, and took the program to earn early release or to spare their families the embarrassment of pubic trial, and because there is little to no chance in this country that the courts will exercise discernment and judicial restraint in their judgments.

Another peculiarity about Missouri sex offender laws involving determination and treatment and/or incarceration: If accused of a sexual offense, the state will *not* pay for or even allow, as far as I witnessed, for the accused to take a polygraph to prove that he did not do what his 'victim' claimed he did. You see, polygraphs are not admissible in a Missouri court of law as evidence. Therefore, their findings are mute, inadmissible.

Here is a further peculiarity, if an accused sex offender completes the MOSOP- agreeing with his victim's account of the alleged offense- he gets early release and a few years on parole. With that parole, he is to participate in court-ordered therapy and *polygraphed* at his or her own expense to *prove* he has not tried to contact and has not seen his alleged victim. That he has not visited parks, playgrounds, pools, schools- anywhere children or teenagers might frequent or hang out.

Furthermore, personal questions are asked about behavior, sexual and otherwise, that may have nothing to do with the alleged crime. If the paroled sex offender fails these polygraphs (and many might simply out of nervousness), it is a ticket back to the penitentiary to walk down the remainder of his sentence. In addition, the failure of a polygraph can be used to place the now labeled *parole-violating* sex offender in the Predator Unit.

Because the Predator Unit is a mental health facility and not 'a prison', the 'resident' may be held there for observation until his dying day. His or her release is solely in the hands of therapists and the sentencing judge. The accused Al-Qaeda terrorist at Guantanamo

Bay has a much better chance of release than those interned in a Predator Unit.

Final observation: The post-prison polygraphs never ask if the paroled sex offender really did sexually abuse or molest the alleged victim. Once charged with an offence, there is little opportunity afforded to prove innocence.

Once again, I am not saying that even a minority of men and women charged with this type of crime are innocent. But I am saying that some of them surely are innocent and plea bargain for a variety of reasons- most to spare their families the humiliation of a public trial and to avoid getting the maximum years 'promised' by the prosecuting attorney. Example: "If you don't accept the seven year sentence, I will charge you with twenty counts instead of one, and you will be looking at thirty to fifty years in prison. So, what's it going to be?"

Many of those charged are not by nature (using its normal not legal definition) violent people, although they will forever be known as violent offenders because of the wording of the laws and the new 'classification' of all sexual offenses as 'violent'. (I acknowledge that most sexual offenses are violent to one degree or another. But how do we classify consensual sex between a teenager and an adult? How can that equate with forcible rape? Is there no distinction to be made between that and forcible rape?)

There is no distinction between consensual sex and forcible rape under the present laws. Furthermore, should not *intent* be a consideration, as well, in sentencing? It is for other crimes. All offenders will forever be registered sex offenders listed on state and national websites available for anyone to read.

So, when the registered man or woman applies to get a loan to go back to school, or to get vocational training, when he tries to get any job, when he seeks to rent a house or apartment, he must admit his 'label' and in most cases will be denied all of the above. If he is hired, it is not long before a coworker or associate looks him up on the internet. Then the harassment begins and management looks for any reason or excuse to dismiss him.

Surely, men in that situation may get help from joining a church. However, when the labeled sex offender does join a church, it is not long before one of the diligent parishioners finds him on the internet. Although the registered sex offender 'always' comes in late, sits in the back away from families, teens and children, and leaves early, his name is whispered in sincere Christian charity to other parishioners, to the youth minister, pastor or priest- you know, for prayer. He is looked upon and treated with suspicion and disdain. "A leper is among us."

The registered sex offender finds even more doors closed to him. If he or she, by nature is a helper, and offers to be a volunteer for a 'Christian' organization, he is rejected. No one wants a registered sex offender volunteer, no matter how 'reformed' and repentant he is- even in a soup kitchen for the homeless. After all, how can one distinguish between 'helping' and 'grooming' behaviors?

Back to Billy

Like all men court-ordered to take the MOSOP, Billy kept a thick manila envelope in his footlocker labeled 'LEGAL'. It contained a copy of the police report of his 'charges'- the account of the alleged crime and the evidence and testimonies against him. (Some men kept several thick envelopes.)

If a convicted sex offender came to FCC without a copy of the police report of his victim's statement, he had to get one. He would not be allowed in the MOSOP without it. Why? Because the 'accused' had to agree, verbatim with the victim's statement as recorded in the police report and as charged by the prosecuting attorney to be allowed to begin and remain in the MOSOP.

Billy asked my assistance in preparing many letters of appeal for him. I read his legal documents several times and the allegations of his ex-wife and the report of the arresting and investigating officers. At first, thinking that Billy was like most cons- that he saw his self as 'not guilty' regardless of the facts- I was very surprised at what I read in the police report. I think you will be too. (Because I do not have the actual report in-hand, I must recount what I read and reread from memory. This of course counts as hearsay. I ask the reader to indulge my memories once again.)

The divorce granted a few months before, the grounds for it was incompatibility. However, Billy told me that he divorced his wife because she had cheated on him with his best friend. He and his ex-wife separated at the time and continued to live separately. He began dating one of his ex-wife's girlfriends. This allegedly upset his ex to no end.

From the police report I read, Billy and his ex-wife agreed upon the following occurrences: She invited him over for supper. He came. After the meal, she questioned him about his relationship with her girlfriend. He admitted to the relationship and further disclosed that they were thinking about getting married. His ex-wife pleaded for him to take her back. He refused and got up to leave.

According to Billy, his ex-wife asked him to stay the night and to have sex with her one last time. He had been partying with her and decided to continue the party in the bedroom, as requested. They had intercourse without using a condom.

Here is where their stories differ. The ex-wife stated to the police that Billy left after supper- no 'sexual' encounter invited or otherwise took place. After she had gone to bed, he returned, broke a pane of glass in a window, let himself in and raped her with a hunting knife to her throat.

Billy stated to the police that his ex, as previously stated, requested sex with him one last time, he obliged, and when she asked him again to take her back, he responded, "I just came for the fuck. There is no way in hell I'd ever take you back," or words to that affect. He then fell asleep naked in her bed. He remained thus until the police arrived the next morning and arrested him for trespassing, forced-entry, and rape using a deadly weapon.

The police report also stated that they found no pane of glass broken in any window or door of the house. Furthermore, they found no knife of any kind in the bedroom, or in Billy's truck, and no knife marks on the ex-wife or any indication on her body or on his or in the room that any kind of struggle had occurred. They found Billy sleeping naked on his stomach as if he did not have a care in the world.

Tried by a jury of his peers, Billy was found guilty on all counts. After all, his semen was in the vagina of his ex-wife- proof positive that he had had sex with her. His distraught ex-wife explained the nonexistent broken pane of glass.

Upon reflection, the ex-wife testified that she was probably too drunk to lock the door after Billy left, and assumed at the time she called the police the next morning that he had broken in. Who cares when and how he got in? The nonexistent knife...Billy must have awakened from a dead drunk in the middle of the night and hid it somewhere, never to be found. Her multitude of tears said it all. Billy's court-appointed defense attorney rarely challenged or questioned any of this.

The reader and I certainly can never know what really happened that fateful night. A few things are clear. Billy was stupid and naïve and violated the cardinal rule in dealing with exes- never have sex with them again. Do not hang out with them.

Regardless of how stupid or naïve the young man was, can *reasonable doubt* be established from what happened that night based on the police report? Evidently, the jury of Billy's peers found no reason to doubt. On the other hand, perhaps their final deliberation was on a Friday, and with the threat of sequestering for the weekend, they found it easier to come to a verdict favorable to the prosecution. After all,

"It is better to be safe than sorry." Surely, this never happens.

It is my understanding of the American system of justice that, with the lives of men and women *hanging in the balance*, the burden rests upon the prosecuting attorney to prove guilt beyond *a reasonable doubt*. The judge cannot lock people up based on circumstantial evidence and the many times contradictory, prejudiced, or coached testimony of victims or witnesses. If there is a reasonable doubt, the jury must acquit.

My introduction to Billy and his case, and to other men like him, would never have taken place apart from the work of a very skilled word weaver, the prosecuting attorney. Weaving circumstantial or flimsy evidence with facts and prejudicial, manufactured, or coached testimony, the prosecutor many times causes the jurors to ignore reasonable doubt and common sense- that is his job, to get a conviction. As the limited but life-altering and life-threatening games played on the prison yard, the court room- American jurisprudence- is a game of power and influence, but with almost limitless scope and consequences.

I will say that again. The judgments of courts- from the Supreme Court of the United States to State Supreme Courts to Criminal courts- are almost limitless in their influence, exercise of power, and consequences. P.A.s and judges are true local (yard) powerbrokers.

Court-appointed defense attorneys and poorly paid defense attorneys therefore, whether in truth or just in perception, are seen as and treated by judges and P.A.s as 'pawns' representing 'pawns'. The jury adopts this perception, I think unconsciously, maybe through the process of courtroom osmosis. After all, there is nothing quite as boring as days and days of courtroom procedure and testimony.

It is understood that being appointed or elected to the office of prosecutor goes hand-in-hand with political ambition. We see it every election cycle- a P.A. of 'many years and experience' running for state Attorney General, for state senator or representative, or for higher office on a platform of 'tough on criminals'. Whether the P.A. is worthy of higher office or not, the juror/electorate unwittingly and most willingly swing the doors to higher office wide-open for him or her.

It is almost as if a few powerful influential word weavers are stepping on (criminalizing) the many just to attain more street-cred and greater power and influence on the yard (society) to advance their own political careers and agendas. Hell, they gobble-up guys like Billy and their poorly-paid pawn attorneys like they were *cucumber on a garden salad*. American Justice is the dressing that goes down with them.

This account of Billy's story is included not to defend him or to champion his innocence. It is simply included to *cause reasonable doubt*. In a court of law common folk are not to "bear false witness," to lie under threat of jail-time for perjury. Is it less a crime to weave words painting a false picture of the defendant in order to sway a jury? Why, it would be like a politician lying to the electorate in order to 'attain' higher office. Surely, this never happens.

Shouldn't the prosecuting attorney's job include searching out the truth and acquitting the innocent, and not just in assuming guilt and finding all guilty and incarcerating them? Why is their title and job description only to find and prove guilt? How many thousands of innocent men and women are in taxpayer-supported jails and prisons, falsely accused, poorly represented?

On the other hand, if Billy had committed past acts of aggression or violence toward his wife, he never shared that with me. If he did commit a rape against his ex-wife, then his prosecution is just and so were the actions of the prosecuting attorney, jury, and judge.

Let me be clear on this point: whether the rape is against an adult or a child, it causes life-long damage to the victim(s). There is not just a loss of dignity or control in rape. Rape is a violation- physical, emotional and mental torture- just short of violent murder in its effect.

Rape is a horrendous violation of the person, demeaning and degrading, taking away their power and right to say *no*. It is a sin against God, nature, society, the victim and collateral victims, and a sin against the rapist's own soul and mind. Under no circumstances is it ever right or to be condoned. It is especially heinous when committed by a trusted and loved family member, neighbor, relative, or caregiver.

Although I have been harsh in my assessment of some prosecuting attorneys and judges, I do realize that many, if not most, are honorable, decent, moral men and women seeking to serve and protect society. For me, this fact alone creates an enormous burden for them to shoulder. *Justice and truth are never self-serving*. The prosecutor and judges must make this clear to a jury. Judgments upon our fellow human beings should only fall if the *evidence* convicts *beyond a reasonable doubt*.

Joey and his motorcycle mama

Lucy was the only woman I wrote to whom I actually met after my stint in prison. She was in her early thirties when we met. She was blonde, well figured, very attractive...until she opened her mouth. It is not what you think. Her teeth were the victim of years of methamphetamine abuse; she had meth-mouth.

Lucy had abused illegal and sometimes legal drugs since she was fourteen. When I met her, she was clean, working full-time as a waitress. Raising her five-year-old son, she cohabited with her husband's best friend, Fred.

Joey was in his late twenties when I met him. He was fit and handsome, blonde, and was the progeny of biker folk. That is what attracted Lucy to him. He was her "Knight on shinning Harley". Joey was raised by parents who were members of a motorcycle club (gang) in Colorado. He was a high school dropout and one of my G.E.D. students.

Stopped for a minor traffic violation, Joey was arrested after it was discovered that he was transporting a trunk full of illegal drugs. Upon his conviction, his best friend and partner raised enough money from the club to move his wife and child to Missouri from Colorado. He rented a two-bedroom house with a small yard near the prison.

During the first years of his incarceration, Joey was housed at The Walls in Jefferson City- a level-five prison with high stone walls. After a few years of good behavior, he was transferred to FCC- a level-four camp with a high-electrified wire fence. There he studied for his G.E.D. Although he had many years to walk down, he determined to reform himself in order to be a good example to his son. His wife, son, and best friend visited every other weekend, and Joey lived for those short visits.

When he first petitioned me for help in writing letters to his wife, Joey made me aware of a problem. Lucy was illiterate. Joey longed to write long emotional letters expressing his love- most with erotic frankness- but he also wanted to write a page to his son and a page or two to his partner.

The letters had to be written in plain simple language, sometimes spelling words phonetically, sometimes drawing a picture after the word. It was imperative that Lucy understand clearly what Joey was saying and feeling- his intent, his love.

Lucy was going to night school. Her goal was to get her G.E.D. in order to help her son with his lessons when he started elementary school. She also took the classes because it helped her feel close to her incarcerated husband. It gave them something of mutual interest to talk about during visits.

For those who are not familiar with the 'biker' culture, let me just add a few clarifying words here. When Joey was arrested, his first phone call was not to a lawyer or to his parents or wife. It was to his best friend and partner, Fred.

Joey directed his partner to take care of his wife and son. In other words, his 'biker brother' was to move in with them and take care of *all* their needs, including sleeping with his wife, until his release.

When I met the very tall Fred, he pulled into the driveway in an old pickup, returning home from doing construction work. He kissed Lucy on the lips at the door, picked up 'the squirt' and twirled him around, then over the shoulder, through the legs, held him straight out, pulled him close and kissed him, then landed him on the front porch into his mother's legs and arms. It was very touching to see. There was no doubt in my mind that Fred was a wonderful loving affectionate surrogate husband and father.

Raised in a predominantly white middle class suburb, you might think that 'biker' culture was as foreign to me as redneck, ghetto, and Hispanic cultures. However, I actually, got a taste of it for a year right next door at the tender age of twelve.

For many years, our next-door neighbors had been a Navy Chief Petty Officer and his wife. When he retired, he bought a home and grocery store/bait shop on the gulf coast. He and his wife left immediately to set up their new life. The Chief called his early thirty-something son in California, and invited him and his girlfriend to 'house sit' for 'a few months'. They ended up living in the house for a year.

When the couple arrived, they did not arrive in a car, truck or van. They arrived on a Chopper with saddlebags. To this day, I think they had a stash of illegal drugs in them and not clothes.

Diggy and Lizzie was an interesting pair. They claimed to belong to a biker gang- a rival of The Hell's Angels. To a twelve-year-old boy, listening to Diggy's stories was like listening to tales of the old west- bar fights, gang wars, and shoot-em-ups. I hung on every word as Gospel.

Quite unexpectedly, I met Lizzie first. My mother, the 'Welcome Wagon' of the neighborhood, sent me with a plate full of fresh-from-the-oven cookies at eleven a.m. on a Sunday morning, to welcome the new neighbors. As I had always done when visiting the Chief, I knocked at the side door under the carport- for quite some time.

Seeing the Chopper nearby under a tarp, I knew the neighbors were home and could not imagine anyone sleeping in so late on a Sunday morning. (I was from a family of early-risers, and had never been introduced to folk who party all night and sleep all the next day...or two...or three.) Finally, the door swung open.

There was Lizzie, a good ten years older than Diggy, wearing her left arm as a bra over her huge boobs. But the first thing I noticed was that she was wearing lacey see-through panties. (Only in a few catalogs had I ever seen a woman in such a state of undress before- not a living breathing one, like now. It was innocence itself staring into the bushy crotch of the sexual revolution amazed and applauding!) Blushing embarrassment, almost choking on my drool, with gaping mouth, I was struck dumb. Diggy, wearing only white briefs arrived right after Lizzie and addressed me.

"Who the hell are you and what are you banging on my door for?" It immediately dawned on me that I had woken up Lizzie.

"Oh, that's the boy from next door. What's up, sport?" Diggy intervened.

In double-embarrassment, I gulped to speak but could not.

"You're going to get a boner if you keep staring at my girlfriend like that. You going to jerk off, or are you going to tell us what you're here for?"

"My mom sent cookies..." I whispered.

"Fuckin'-A, thank your mom for the breakfast," Diggy responded, digging in.

I forced the plate of cookies toward Lizzie, knowing that I would get a complete show that I could tell the other neighborhood boys about, if she took it with her left hand. Diggy saw right through me and quickly sidestepped in front of Lizzie and took the plate. He then leaned down and whispered.

"You little freak, I'll bet you've never been this close to pussy before. Come back this evening around six. We'll talk."

The door closed and I turned to go home. Then I remembered my lines.

"Welcome to the neighborhood!" I yelled.

During our first meeting, Diggy told me about his biker background, bragged that Lizzie could shoplift a dozen eggs in her bra, (I still find that hard to believe, wondering where she found the room.) and divulged that he was a pharmacist, but did not have a license to practice in his present state. It was all believable...to a twelve-year-old boy.

After several rides on the back of his Chopper, and a few more glimpses of Lizzie and Diggy in a state of immodesty...even in bed...Diggy pulled me aside and asked if I would be his 'delivery boy'. I would deliver lunch sacks of pharmaceuticals on my bike and bring back envelopes with payment. Then I would get a nice tip. That year I cleaned up on that deal and spent a lot of time with a couple that had no *plex* about parading around in partial-nudity.

Our new neighbors soon hosted a few very loud all-night parties. My brother and I shared a bedroom, and our window gave us a clear view of the partiers coming and going. We saw and heard everything. During the second party, we dressed and snuck out.

The biker partiers accepted us as if we were their pets or mascots. The heavy metal music, the sight of scantily clad women, the overpowering aroma of pot, and the sight of bongs and blunts and a water pipe from India, and plastic bags of pharmaceuticals, of couples 'coupling' everywhere was a revelation. We gaped in awe at all we witnessed but tried to act cool.

My brother began his drinking days then. I snuck an upper at the first party we attended and a few more thereafter and loved the feelings I got from them. Soon after, my brother and I bought a black light, a fake skull, a myriad of 'The Grateful Dead' posters, and hung an American flag upside down with a peace symbol over the star field in our bedroom.

We wanted to be cool like our neighbors. We begged our parents to let us grow our hair long. Most boys at school and in the neighborhood had long hair.

Neighbors called the police on a few occasions. Mom eventually called Diggy's mom and the parties came to an abrupt halt. That was the sum and total of my experience with biker folk.

Sitting down with Fred and Lucy in their living room, I immediately noticed a coffee table full of children's Bible storybooks. Lucy stated that she and Fred read a story to her son every night before bedtime. (The squirt's favorite was *Zacchaeus and the Sycamore tree*.) She did not want him to grow up without God, as she had. Her son played quietly in a corner with his red fire engine.

Fred and Lucy were open about their understanding of their relationship. He would provide for her and 'the squirt' and be a husband and father until Joey got out of prison. Then he would move out. The arrangement was as simple as that, and he had done it before for Joey and Lucy and for a few other biker brothers.

Pointing out that Joey would be in prison at least fifteen years, I asked Fred how he could so easily bow out and move out for Joey. Surely, his emotional attachment and affections would grow for Lucy and her son. Joey's son would, more and more see Fred as his true father.

Fred looked over at Lucy, squeezed her hand and answered with a benign, "Joey's my partner. It's the way it is. It's the way it has to be; that's all."

Later on, Fred took me into the backyard and showed me his Chopper under a tarp. It was badass. Observing my keen interest, he showed me his leather jacket with his club's emblem on the back, his 'ink', and photos of him and his club, of Joey and Lucy back in Colorado. They were from a very large extended family that lived in a sort of self-sustaining community.

Why did Joey ask me to visit his wife, Fred, and his son? He wanted me, in person, to read Lucy the love story that I had written in prison. It was the story of what should have been, until it all went wrong. Sometimes a quality seen as a detraction by some is an attraction to someone else. Joey's intent in becoming a drug mule was based not in love of lucre. It was for love of Lucy.

You see, when Joey was in his mother's womb, her body demanded so much calcium that it drained her teeth to supply it to Joey. Although she took supplements, she lost her teeth and eventually had to get false ones. While other boys and girls around him had mothers with real teeth and smiles, Joey's beautiful mother had sacrificed hers for him. Her genuine smile came from false teeth. But it was years before his father could afford them.

Joey always remembered this. It always touched a chord in him. It was one of the things that drew him to Lucy in the first place. She had ruined her teeth and needed new ones. He wanted to restore her beauty and dignity- to be her Knight on shinning Harley.

Joey carried (muled) drugs in order to make money to buy his wife new teeth. He also wanted to give her and their son a new start- a new life somewhere. At the time, he was thinking that he didn't want his son growing up in the biker culture as he had- one toe just over the line of what most honest folk call 'legal'. Just one major illegal act (score) and he could accomplish one absolute good for his family.

Judges and juries do not look at it that way- the P.A. and judge use 'legal-speak' to explain the 'crime' and motive. The deeply personal reasons and motivations of the defendant are dismissed as *irrelevant*. Putting aside the crime committed, may I ask the reader a question?

Are the lives of bikers less relevant or are they worth less than yours or mine? Just because they come from a different perhaps more coarse piece of cloth, it does not mean that they are not cloth. I must borrow from the great bard again, this time from the *Merchant of Venice*, Act III, scene I.

Hath not a (biker) eyes? Hath not a (biker) hands, organs, dimensions, senses, affections, passions; fed with the same food, hurt with the same weapons, subject to the same diseases, heal'd by the same means, warm'd and cool'd by the same winter and summer as a Christian is? If you prick us, do we not bleed? If you tickle us, do we not laugh? If you poison us, do we not die? And if you wrong us, shall we not revenge? If we are like you in the rest, we will resemble you in that.

Joey, Lucy, and 'the squirt' and tens of thousands like them do not seek revenge. They simply want to be together again- a united loving family. Joey and Lucy came to understand by painful experience the destructiveness of drug abuse in their own lives and got treatment. They have since attended N.A. and A.A. meetings.

Joey's judgment clouded when offered a lot of 'freedom' money to mule drugs from Colorado to Chicago. I surely did not think I was doing anything illegal or destructive when I, at the age of twelve, muled for Diggy. It may be a poor comparison, and I am not defending Joey's crime or crimes like it. However, I think the reader gets my meaning and intent.

Many good people, who may be infinitely different from you, have the same dreams, hopes, and fears. They simply lack the same opportunities that you have had.

They want to provide for their families and sometimes turn to illegal means to do it.

They are the *Jean Valjeans* of the *Les Miserables*. I have witnessed many times biker folk, whom some consider the 'miserable ones,' show more empathy, compassion and humanity toward their fellow human beings than the most devoted ardent well-dressed churchgoers.

Was it the righteous, the finely dressed good citizen, the priest, that aided the man after his cruel beating and robbery on the Jericho road? No. It was the hated half-breed, the Samaritan, who showed goodness and kindness, who went out of his way to pay for the man's treatment asking no remuneration in return. He restored dignity with wholeness to a man beaten almost to death.

"Judge not, that ye be not judged." "Do unto others as you would have them do unto you." "Love your neighbor as yourself."

Do these precepts come from a mere Bible Story book of a child? Have they any place or consideration in a court of law or in a jury's deliberation? Alternatively, should those honorable men and women pulled unwillingly from their beds consider only, "An eye for an eye, a tooth for a tooth?"

Those questions must be answered by another: "Lord, who is my neighbor?"

These days we do not take the time to get to know our neighbor, much less their true hopes, dreams, and needs. Perhaps if the righteous and rich in our society answered that one question proactively, many acts of crime, not to mention wars, would be prevented and many lives saved from ruin. However, it seems the only goal of most of the rich in our society is to be self-serving and not to serve their fellow man.

(The reader will find the story of Joey in part two entitled, Joey and Lucy, a love story made right. I caution that it is, as Joey desired it. I would rate some of it NC-17.)

Old-G, Pops

A few days before I transferred to Church Farm, I was summoned to a 'sit-down'. After four-plus years, Old-G wanted a 'sit-down'. The Great Man of the yard, who rarely left his housing unit, the Grand Puppeteer, the Wizard behind the curtain wanted to talk with me.

What did he want of me? Surely, it was a favor- some task performed on the outside, some message delivered, perhaps to his mother; a message he did not trust others to carry. That is what immediately came to mind the sleepless night before the meet.

'He's old, maybe dying. Maybe he is going to tell me his story at long last.' That had to be it. What else could it be? I was on pins and needles. Here is what I remember of the meeting.

Old-G looked average for a man of his age. He was in his early seventies, had white hair and a spare tire around his waist. He looked nonthreatening except for the decades of fading prison ink painted on his arms, neck, ankles, and I am sure everywhere else on his body. It was as if the curtain had been thrown open revealing an ordinary magician behind the specter of a powerful wizard.

I did not let my senses deceive me. His two teardrop tattoos were from murder in the first-degree. He was serving two life sentences for killing his wife and her lover. Who knows what atrocities he had committed in prison to attain and keep his position as Old-G?

There was no formal introduction. Old-G sat down near me on the bleachers and studied me a moment through dark sunglasses. He removed them and asked a question.

"You know what you leave here with, young man?"

"I'm really not sure," I replied.

"You leave here with my respect and the respect of a lot of the men- many of them my boys."

"I'm sorry, I don't follow," I responded.

"You treated every man as equal. I have rarely seen that in here. It did not matter their race, religion, or crime; you helped men that came to you inside school and out.

"I heard about you tutoring men on your own time on the yard, in the library and gym. You went out of your way to figure out how to teach them in a way they could understand. I've never known a tutor to do that. It earned you a lot of respect and protection."

"I never knew that," was my response in hushed humility.

"The one word you almost never hear in here is, 'thanks'. You know that. Instead you hear, 'Right-on' or 'Cool'. That is about all you are going to get from gangstas and cons.

"But I want to extend my hand and thanks to you. You never lost who you really are. But then, you only had a nickel to walk down. You weren't here long enough to lose who you are."

Reflecting on what Old-G was saying, I saw the truth of it, but I did not know how to respond. He did not offer his hand then. He studied me again. I braced myself for 'the parting favor' he was about to ask of me. It never came.

"Gabriel is one of my boys. I don't mean that like it sounds- not in a prison sense. I regard him and many others as my sons or grandsons. Few know this, and it is not advertised, but they call me 'Pops'.

"Have you ever known an old fag to be called or regarded as a grandfather or father on the yard?"

I had never entertained the question. Upon reflection, I had never heard an old homosexual called by anything but his name or by some expletive or worse.

"Men usually call straight old men 'Pops' or 'Granddad' in here. It is the ultimate title of respect, for me, anyway.

"These boys are the only family I have left. I'll die in here surrounded by many of them. I love them all.

"You taught and helped many of my sons in here get their G.E.D. I want to thank you for that. Also, I'm curious to know what you learned from them."

Breathing in deeply, I pondered the question. What had I learned from the men for whom I had tutored and written letters and love stories? It was an introspective question I had not yet considered. What was the common denominator of the men I had gotten to know?

"I learned that most of them are poets. Whether they have the education to express their feelings and thoughts or not, it seems most write poems or song lyrics. Life is poetry."

Many of them, like Gabriel, checked out guitars from the gym music room and created music to express their souls in song.

"You're right. Most are sometime poets, at least the younger fellas. Don't ever forget that. In this place and many hundreds like it, a man expresses his humanity through poetry.

"It could be art, or songs, or in verse; it's all poetry of the soul. We are all weavers of words like you, many just not as polished. We all have a story to tell.

"And what did you discover about the people on the outside- the people who have never been incarcerated?"

"That's easy. I learned that they can't read between the lines."

"Well said. That covers a lot of ground. Elaborate."

"A fish writes home asking mom and dad for some extra money to buy new sneakers or shorts or socks or a sweatshirt. Many times he is really asking for money to buy a carton or two for his or his cellie's or a partner's protection.

"He writes that he's been moved to a new cell or to the other side of the camp. He doesn't know why. Between the lines he's saying that he's threatened by or was raped or beaten by his cellie and is trying to spare himself a second rape or beating.

"I did that at first; I paid Henry for protection."

"I know. Who do you think gets that second carton of cigarettes?"

Old-G winked, and I realized how much I truly did not know about power on the yard. I did not know its workings or 'the power' behind the powerbrokers. It never dawned on me that they had to pay for that right- the right to charge others for protection. Truly, the wise man knows that he does not know. I was not wise.

"What else did you learn about the folks on the other side of the razor wire?" Old-G asked.

"That life for many on the outside is a resume. But for most of us, now me included, it's not. Also, I think that whatever happens to me from here on out will depend on the goodness of the people of Missouri," I answered solemnly and tearfully.

"Son, in here you can buy protection. Not out there. In here, you can always have someone watching your back. Not out there. In here, there is some sense of comradeship. There's the code and a clear set of rules.

"As a felon, out there you will find none. You will not be given any benefit of the doubt. They will see you as an enemy or a threat. Your life before the penitentiary does not exist. It does not matter or factor into the equation of your new reality.

"Everything will be hard to come by. It's every man for his self, especially for those just released. You gotta keep that in your head at all times. Do you have family to help you once you leave Church Farm?"

"No, I'll be going to a halfway house in St. Louis. I've never lived there before. I got no one there," I answered, feeling sad.

"You sure won't get any help from anyone in here. We do not expect any from you. You'll be starting with nothing, at the bottom of the barrel. All I can wish you is good luck...I think you've found more goodness in here than you'll find out there."

Old-G extended his hand and shook mine- a very rare occurrence and rarely seen on the yard. I teared up. I felt like I was leaving family. Old-G got up and turned to walk away.

"Thanks for the heads-up, Pops."

Old-G paused, looked back, nodded his appreciation and approval, and donned his sunglasses.

Leaving FCC, I felt a sense neither of relief, nor of bitterness. I felt anxious, fearful, and sad. I expected Gabriel to meet with me one last time, so I could thank him. It was understood; he did not owe me; I did not owe him. We would never have been friends (partners) on the inside, nor would we ever have been friends on the outside.

I changed from prison grey into orange coveralls. Shackled, I stepped onto the bus feeling a sense of thankfulness with many stories to tell. However, I did not have the energy or desire to tell them then, and I barely do now.

Church Farm, Ricky, and the halfway house

The last few months of my prison experience were spent at a very old level-two prison; I believe now closed down. Upon my arrival, it was truly a culture shock. Everything was the exact opposite of FCC- everything.

Shackled and descending the bus steps wearing the traditional orange coveralls, we looked for the yard. There was not one, visible anyway. We were unshackled right there by the bus on open ground. No guards, no gun towers, no razor wire, no electric fence was visible. The CO bus drivers opened the storage compartment and we collected our TVs, fans, sacks of clothes and essentials, put them on rolling carts and walked toward an open double door.

A CO greeted us and beckoned us to follow him down the hall. That is when I knew I had metaphorically left the black and white world of Kansas tornado country and stepped into the colorful Land of *Oz*, but minus the wicked witch and flying monkeys. There in the broad hallway were tables bolted to the floor like at FCC but with men seated at each one holding carving knives, handsaws, and sandpaper. All of the men dressed in street clothes, but with I.D. badges dangling from cuffs.

Looking back at the open double doors, I waited for them to magically slam shut and lock with a loud metal thud and pop, or for the CO to order us to stop so he could shut and lock them. (There was the outside world with highways and farm roads within easy walking distance. There were trees and weeds and flowers and gravel and birds and squirrels. I could see them. I could smell them- close enough to run back and touch.) An *inmate* got up and shut the doors behind us!

Amazed, I stared at him. He was six-foot-four, skinny as a rail, and smiled big as he walked back to his table to collect his birdhouse and tools. (Most inmates there made birdhouses to sell at local craft fairs.) He passed us and headed to the hobby room. We continued to walk down the hall until we got to the property room where we registered our possessions and surrendered our coveralls for uniforms. We were then led to one of the open bays.

It was not immediately apparent. Having never been to Church Farm, I did not know its design. Four main buildings were set in a square with a small yard in the middle. Even in inclement weather, inmates could walk anywhere they needed to be without getting rained on or snowed on or putting on a coat.

Many of the inner walls had professional quality murals painted by skilled resident inmate artists. I remember a section of cinder block wall of an African theme with Elephants, Zebras, Lions, Water Buffalo, and an undersea theme with sunken ships, Sea Horses and treasure chest. Projecting out from the main buildings were four two-story wings with bays of bunk beds.

There was no CO pod in sight. Upon entering the bay, one CO greeted us sitting at a desk in the front. He checked his floor plan and had a 'resident' lead us to our cubicles. (The man who shut the double doors, who returned his birdhouse and tools to the hobby room, magically appeared and volunteered to lead me to my bunk. I think he got a kick out of seeing the shock and awe on the faces of new arrivals.) I immediately associated and compared the place to the Texas jails I had seen on TV in late 1997. There were one hundred residents occupying that one cramped open-air space.

Each cubicle housed a bunk bed and desk, with two foot lockers beside it. There was exactly eighteen inches between bunk bed and desk. I did observe that there were a few men, like my soon-to-be tour guide, on single beds, not bunk beds. They were the honor residents. You had to be a long-timer and work on maintenance or at another support job to get those beds.

I was a newbie, so I got top billing, as Ricky referred to it. (At FCC, the premium bunks were the top bunks. At Church Farm, they were the bottom bunks- a little more privacy.)

After storing my gear, Ricky walked me through the bay. Cubicles with bunk beds were stationed on each windowed wall- it was an old prison with outer walls of about five feet with large windows above them measuring about ten or twelve feet. In the middle of the cramped bay were more bunk bed cubicles.

Ricky cautioned me to be very careful descending from my lofty perch. "Make sure your bunk mate knows you're coming down," he warned. "Step on the desk first, then the foot locker next to it while holding onto your bed," he further advised. (Good advice for living in a very narrow space)

Completing our round and a few introductions, Ricky led me out of the bay without checking in with the CO, without being called out. I had never seen that before. In a level-four camp, you only left your cell for assigned work, or during open wing or yard, or when the 'Goon Squad' arrived dressed in riot control gear (usually quarterly) to tear apart cells and do cavity searches right there in the open bay on inmates stripped down to their briefs, lined up along and facing walls. There was no such thing as 'free movement'.

Ricky took me to the hobby room, more introductions, to the cafeteria complete with salad bar, to the other bays, to the store, the library, and finally to the enclosed yard. We immediately took a seat on the bleachers for a chat. Some things never change.

We watched inmates playing softball on the very small ball field. (I wondered if any windows were ever shattered accidentally by a homerun ball.) It was then that I noticed, that on the other side of the four walls of windows, were the hallways we had just walked. Cool.

We did not have time to size each other up at the bleachers. That would come later during longer talks. I immediately pegged Ricky as a player. He wanted something from this short-timer. A few months later, he stole one thing and I freely gave him the other.

It was count time. What do I do? By then I had met my bunkmate. He was in his mid-twenties, and like me, waiting to get his walking papers. He was cordial. He directed me to sit on my bunk for count. (I expected that we would be ordered to stand at the end of our bunks with I.D. badges visible.)

The CO came around with his roster and counted everyone, as they were- some men watching their TVs or listening to radios or playing cards. It was all so surreal. Count time at Church Farm was a mere but necessary inconvenience.

Dinnertime came at last! I expected the same fare I had gotten used to at FCC- a small bland portion of breaded mystery meat and refried fries or mashed potatoes from a box, or at breakfast, powered eggs and soy bacon and sausage or cereal. Dinner- all meals really- was the most shocking thing I discovered about Church Farm.

First, it was designated 'Dinner' or 'the Evening meal', not 'chow time'. As each bay of men lined up, we were given our portions of meat and fries, and whatever, by happy smiling servers. This was weird. But then I looked at my plate. It was *half-full* of real carved roast beef. The other half of the plate was soon filled with French fries. They used a *cereal bowl* to scoop the fries! At FCC, they used an 8oz serving cup.

Beside all that, you could have as many slices of bread as you wanted, and the salad bar was heaven. It had everything you could possibly want to put in and on a salad. Again, take what you can eat- no limits. I had not seen a salad bar in almost five years! Of course, Ricky was there as tour guide drinking in my amazed, "Ooos, and aahs." Then I discovered real sweet tea, not some form of generic fruity-tasting drink.

Nearing the end of the meal, I found myself full for the first time since my incarceration. A CO walked to the front of the serving line. Ricky said, "Watch this."

"Seconds; boys come and get your seconds. Don't want any of this food going into the garbage cans!"

I never heard that at FCC. With all my heart, I wanted to jump up and race with the younger fellas to the serving line again. But I was too full to move an inch. Ricky, having a high metabolism, jumped up, got his second plate full, returned and gobbled it all down laughing at me. Suddenly, the cramped bays did not seem so bad.

Upon our return to the bay, before entering, Ricky directed me into an open doorway containing a dressing room and then a dark blue room with dim lighting. He introduced me to six shower stalls- three on one side, three on the other. They were open, so you could view from your stall the three on the other side of the small room. There were no curtains.

To supplement his small state stipend for being the janitor of our bay, Ricky made his living wage partly by rolling unfiltered cigarettes. He, like many poor men I knew at FCC, bought pouches of tobacco and rolling papers at the store, rolled them, and sold them in empty cigarette boxes collected from trash cans. He was quite good at it. He rolled a few hundred a day and made a tidy profit.

The only difference between the smokers of rolled cigarettes at FCC and Church Farm- and I expected just the opposite or the same- was that at FCC the rolling papers were also used to roll joints. I never once smelled pot at Church Farm. Surely, it was there, too.

At FCC, it was almost a weekly occurrence. If you got close enough to men smoking on the bleachers you could smell the pot. From a distance, a CO would assume the inmates were smoking rolled unfiltered cigarettes, or they just did not care what was smoked.

Inmates at FCC would smoke their 'cap' after lights out and count time, blowing the distinctive smoke out the windows. (A lip-balm tube cap was used to measure the pot for sale. Thus, the designation of the pot smoked in a joint as a *cap*.)

[As I write this, I recall the many times Goon Squads tore apart our cells at FCC looking for pot or shanks or other contraband. Each house had lookouts. Any pot or other drugs were flushed before the searches began, before the officers in black riot gear had stepped foot onto the yard. The searches were an inconvenience and treated by inmates as an inside joke. All inmates knew that the pot and shanks were buried on the yard, and only small quickly disposable amounts were kept in the housing units.]

My five months at Church Farm was relaxing and therapeutic. Because it was an honor camp, most men were to be released within a few days, weeks or months. They did not want to do anything that would prolong their prison stay. There were no gangs, obvious threatening pimps, no contracts, no fights, and no shankings. The atmosphere and demeanor of COs and men was casual and cordial- respectful of the peace.

Many inmates enjoyed weekend visits with their loved ones outside of the complex, in front of the administration building. There, support inmates supplied charcoal for barbeque pits. Inmate's families brought chicken, steak, hamburgers, hot dogs, whatever, and grilled right there in front of the prison, spending the whole day with loved ones. Their children played with the other children and ran around freely on the lawn. The experience was surely wonderful, especially for the long-timers. It was restored dignity.

Eventually, I became part of a maintenance crew that voluntarily picked up trash blown onto the grounds. Of course, Ricky volunteered to help out, too. In one of the culverts of the prison property, he introduced me to a 'rascally' raccoon and its family. We studied them and fed them. They dipped each French fry in a bowl of water that we daily provided, and happily ate. No CO attended us. It was a taste of freedom and fun.

Ricky eventually told me his story. He looked younger, but he was a man in his mid-thirties. He received a twenty-plus year sentence for armed robbery and assault. In prison, he was made a prostitute and had been an inmate in several Missouri prisons. At Church Farm he continued to ply his trade, but without having to serve a pimp. He was his own man.

About a month after we met, Ricky showed me the 'reserved' room with a 'Glory Hole' where he plied his trade. Using their woodworking tools, men took a sheet of plywood, cut a few holes wide enough, and positioned to parallel a man's crotch area. It was a place of business. Ricky or one of the other gay men would kneel behind the plywood partition and anonymously service clients. I need not say more.

Ricky also pointed out that less anonymous services were available in the back of our bay as was gambling. Far from the prying eyes of the CO, men were serviced for a price with top bunk inmates used as lookouts. I would imagine that this mostly occurred at night. Men freely walked the bay and went to the bathroom through a door just opposite the shower area.

Once an hour the CO would stretch and walk his post visible to all top bunk inmates. He would rarely question why a man was up or out of bed. As long as you were 'doing no harm' to yourself or someone else, who cares why you are roaming- just stay in the bay. Inmates were in charge of 'neighborhood watch' and God help the thief. Bars of soap or batteries in athletic socks took care of the thieves.

Ricky was one of the most interesting men I had met in prison. He was always joyful and helpful. It was his nature. It was the part of himself he refused to surrender to his reality. However, he did suffer from depression. I found him a few times on his bunk crying into pillow- an attractive young man, whom he adored, had rejected him.

The man also wept for his coming release in a few years. He was terrified at the prospect. His only contacts in the outside world were a few former ex-lovers and a Presbyterian woman, with whom he corresponded, via the phone. Introduced by another released inmate, with whom he spoke with monthly.

Ricky hoped, upon his release to a halfway house, that the woman would assist him in getting a state I.D. and in finding a job. I had not thought that far into the future. Who would help me get those things?

A few final notes about Church Farm: Behind the prison was a Quonset hut just like the ones I saw at the Reception and Diagnostic Center. It housed inmates on work release. They ate breakfast and dinner in the prison, but were given huge sack lunches to take to their outside jobs. At their outside jobs, they made a real salary.

Most of their money went into savings so that, upon their release, they could rent an apartment, maybe even buy a car. They were allowed to keep some money to buy essentials, clothes, shoes, CDs, whatever. I envied them. Their deal was much better than mine- released to a halfway house in a strange city with no help in finding a job, or an apartment, or transportation. At least they got a leg-up before their release.

Church Farm also afforded me another healing opportunity. Once every two weeks I spoke with a Master Level Social Worker. She was empathetic, kind, knowledgeable, genuine; nurturing. I only wish I could have taken her with me upon my release. She would have been an invaluable support system for me. The Social Workers at FCC seemed to focus on 'shame' therapy. It seemed the zeitgeist of the whole camp.

Question: It is held as almost psychological dogma that men and women who turn to crime or drug abuse or who become prostitutes, suffer from low self-esteem. How then can 'shame-based' therapy help to rehabilitate them? How can making them confess at the beginning of each group therapy session that they are monsters, facilitate rehabilitation? How can that help them salvage what little conscience they may have left, or to become empathetic human beings, functional in society?

Shame-based *therapy* reinforces the negative self-talk, the feelings of worthlessness and despair that drive these people to create victims like themselves. Shame-based therapy focuses on the deviant antisocial behaviors and does not aide in creating empathy for victims. I received more valuable counsel in the ten sessions with that one Church Farm social worker than I did from any therapy I received at FCC.

****

The time came. I was released from Church Farm on a state holiday. A few days before, informed of my leaving, I freely paid a carton of premium cigarettes and had my TV taken off my property list and put on Ricky's. It was against the rules- one toe just over the line of what honest folk call legal- but it made him very happy.

I could not have done that at FCC. The bay CO did not really care how the TV materialized in Ricky's cubicle. He just afforded a funny 'you owe me' nod toward him.

Ricky escorted me to the 'closed' property room. It was a state holiday, as I said. No boxes were available to pack the three pair of new jeans and shirts, two belts and dress shoes and new coat sent to me by friends to wear in the real world upon my release. I triple-dressed and sadly left over half my property at Church Farm including books and personal papers. This was my only complaint and disappointment as I left. I entered feeling human and left an overlooked cog.

I received my first and only kiss from an inmate, as I left Church Farm. (The reader must understand this about men kissing men in prison. Even heterosexual men who used gay men for sex usually did not kiss them on the mouth. They wore this distinction like a badge of honor. No one wanted a write-up and go to the hole for that infraction.)

As the CO led Ricky and me to the door leading outside to the waiting cab, he handed over a ticket for my Greyhound bus ride to St. Louis. While I paused to thank the CO and took my last breath of prison air, Ricky grabbed my well-padded arms and planted one right on my lips. The CO shook his head in dismay.

Ricky tearfully laughed holding his skinny belly. I waved a final blushing goodbye. Maybe he saw me as yet 'another' who had gotten away. I was, in a way, flattered, but in hindsight, I think he was just being 'Ricky' and thanking me for the TV. It was his way.

The cab driver was about fifty. He was friendly, cordial. He did not need to ask, "Where to?" The ride for me and for many hundreds of others like me was prearranged by the State of Missouri.

"Did you learn your lesson, son?" asked the cab driver.

Tearfully I answered, "I learned that whatever happens to me after this depends on the goodness of the people of Missouri."

"Them and the good Lord," he responded.

My driver went silent and so was I for the remainder of the ride to the Greyhound bus station in Jefferson City. As I learned from the judicial process and prison, silence can be deafening- so deafening that it leads to deep depression, self-doubt, and quiet debilitating despair. (That is the Post Traumatic Stress talking.)

During my over-dressed bus ride and upon my arrival in St. Louis, I felt hopeless, fearful, on the verge of a tearful breakdown. I knew no one there- just a few ex-cons. How long would I stay at the CO-run honor center before I found a job, had enough money for an apartment, let alone for a car? I had no money except about $18 from the state. It was a state holiday; I had no access to the fifty or so dollars on my books.

Upon my arrival at the Greyhound station in St. Louis, I called the honor center; a car came, and drove me straight to it. It was a mini FCC. It even had razor wire at the top of the walls. I was processed, my fan and cassette player/radio was confiscated (I should have given those to Ricky, too). I was shown to my new cell and introduced to my crack-head cellie. (I'm not lying. He smoked it right there in the room.)

Thereafter, informed that I had a 48-hour Pass to visit family and friends, get a motel room, or to explore downtown St. Louis, the thrilling prospect depressed me even more. I left for six hours and walked the endless cluttered streets, only stopping at a fast food restaurant. The chocolate ice cream tasted good.

When I returned that evening, I was given a phone number to call- a number I didn't recognize. A woman had left a message for me to call her- a name I did not recognize. I called.

It was Gabriel's grandmother. He had called her and told her my parole date. She and Herbie had made some calls and had a staff person at the honor center inform them when they knew my arrival date. I was in shock. Behind razor wire fence, my prostitute angel had done me a 'solid', was still watching my back. Overcome and choked with emotion, I tried to say hello.

Although she was very ill, yiayia arranged for one of her lady friends from church to pick me up the next day for lunch at her expense. Ruth was in her early eighties, married, and in very good health and humor. She handed me a driving manual- from Herbie, who was at work.

Dropping me off later at the honor center, Ruth said she would pick me up in a week- on my next 24-hour leave- for lunch and to take me to get my driver's license, offering to let me first practice-drive her Audi just to get me used to traffic again. "After all, you can't get a job without some form of I.D.," she said. As promised, Ruth did just that. She was such a gracious kind soul- a true Christian, if ever there was one. I did find driving in city traffic nerve wracking and still do.

I was not invited to personally meet Gabriel's family or Herbie. Later, I realized that it was part of the code. After all, no inmate allowed another inmate to insinuate themselves into their family's lives or business from inside or outside of the razor wire. Nevertheless, I am grateful to them and to Ruth for the help and moral support they offered upon my arrival in St. Louis. Joy sprang from sadness; hope sprang from fear.

The last ten-plus years have been hard. Being labeled a felon, violent- a monster- and treated as one at every job interview, is a hard pill to swallow, an enduring reminder and added humiliation. As on the prison yard, I keep my head low, mind my own business, and watch my back. Jobs have been hard to come by; I will not lie to you. At best, they are temporary, handyman jobs with low pay and no benefits. In the present economy, it has gotten doubly hard.

As Old-G wisely warned, my college education, my skills, my resume from former careers are meaningless. I have joined the permanent underclass created by the American Justice System, the disenfranchised.

Do I deserve it? You are the judge and jury of that. I try not to think about it. When I do think about my alleged crime (may I take the luxury of using legal-speak here?), I am truly sorry for it and for its victims and unintended victims.

When I think back on my prison experience, I am truly humbled and grateful for the many good men I met. I feel the utmost empathy for those who had violence done to them, have turned violent, or had to use violence to survive; also for their victims.

What is left of my more personal prison story? What else can this weaver of words say about his crime and time? You will have to read between the lines for that or wait for the whip to drive me to write again. I really do not have the kind of 'guts' required to overcome and write in detail about that...yet. It is mostly vinegar.

Like my evolved and enlightened view of the Missouri and American systems of justice, my view of 'second chances' and of 'society's goodness' has evolved. I unwillingly and sorrowfully find that Old-G was right after all.

For now, there are the love stories. Let me here keep my promises. I begin with the love story of Randy and Millie set in the fantasy land of Royaume'el.

I.
I am.
I am here.
I have wronged.
I am wronged.
I am relevant.
I am here.
I am
I.

Part Two: The Honey

The Boy Monk and the Acolyte

The sound of restless complaint filled the air from birds disturbed by a sudden roll of thunder. It awakened M'Illie. Alighting bed, she walked barefoot across the cool stone floor of the tiny cell of the nunnery and peeked out the stone-latticed portal. It was dawn and a storm was brewing. It was also the time of first-prayer.

She quickly donned habit and joined the procession of acolytes in the hallway drawn by devotion to holy prayer and hunger to humble breakfast. This had been her daily routine since she was twelve. M'Illie was now fifteen.

Just as breakfast ended and the acolytes began preparations for their daily work and study, the Mother Superior was summoned to the outer wall gate. A logger and his son had happened upon a gruesome scene on the forest road. Seeing threatening sky, they thought it prudent to return home.

However, something in a lightening flash captured the logger's vision just around the bend of the road. There, they found an entourage of young monks with an old man robbed and dead- all save one. They conveyed him to the nearby nunnery. It was the boy's only hope for healing, for life.

"Quickly...quickly...gently...men, carry the young man to the priest's guesthouse. We shall forthwith attend. Have you bound wounds? Is there issue of blood?" asked Mother Superior in anxious prying- hands parted from prayer, ready to do God's work.

"No bleeding, Reverend Mother, but for the gash on the forehead; I'd imagine bruising. A deep sleep has taken him," answered the equally anxious logger.

The logger and son lifted the boy monk from their oxcart and carried him across the yard to the guesthouse. Mother followed taking keys from her belt to unlock the door. Inside, averting holy eyes, she had logger and son remove the cloak and disrobe the boy for examination, place him on the priest's bed, leaving only common-cloth tunic, common loin cloth, and long arm-length white gloves upon him.

Rolling the boy over, they lifted the tunic, and found bruising on back and shoulders and on the sides of his tall frame. He was as white as milk, oddly bore no tonsure, and was no more than sixteen, the logger reckoned- about the age of his son, E'Rik.

"The boy may suffer broken ribs, Mother," forewarned the logger.

"Remove the tunic and gloves. I will bind him fast," Mother directed.

It was when the tunic and gloves were removed that a remarkable sight was unveiled to all. Beginning on the fingertips and thumb of the left underhand and flowing across palm and wrist, up the underarm, across the left shoulder, covering chest, flowing again over right shoulder and down the underarm, across right wrist and palm to right thumb and fingertips were inscribed ancient secret sacred runic symbols. Upon seeing them, the logger immediately swore and apologized; Mother Superior beckoned father and son to look away and covered the boy with a blanket.

"God's thanks for your troubles gentlemen. Now on your way," Mother Superior directed.

"But Mother, what could they mean?" E'Rik the younger asked after a gasp and a gulp.

"'Tis not meant to be seen by any but wizards. We were never meant to see it. You must not tell a soul what you have witnessed this day. Those runes have been forbidden by the king. Do you understand, boy?"

"We understand, great Mother. We saw nothing," E'Rik the elder replied. Logger and son took their leave to retrieve the dead and arrange for their burial.

After cleaning the head wound and gently but firmly sewing up the forehead gash, Mother Superior had her most trusted acolyte, M'Illie, prepare stripped cloth to bind the boy monk's ribs. While lifting the sleeping young man to a sitting position and holding him, M'Illie too observed the runic sign, but wisely and prudently declined comment. Once the binding was done, Mother and acolyte gently lowered the boy monk back in recline.

"God's thanks girl; now to your chores and prayers," directed Mother, as she dabbed her brow of sweat.

M'Illie bowed and withdrew in silent obedience as she had learned to do.

Once the acolyte had withdrawn closing the bedroom door behind her, the Mother Superior paused briefly to look reflectively upon the boy, then took the boy's heavy long hooded cloak in-hand and searched it, feeling the outer hems.

Had the robbers found the true treasure? No. There it was, deftly sewn into the cloak behind the thick left embroidered outer hem. Mother replaced it to the chair where she found it and withdrew, hands joined in rosaried-prayer.

****

It was three days before the fevered boy awoke. While asleep, gentle hands tended gentle lips several gentle sips of water. Mother appeared several times daily unannounced to clean the young man, if necessary. When attending him, she paused to study his features as if repressed memories were calling to her from them.

M'Illie was assigned to watch the boy. Once he awoke, she was not to speak with him. She was to summon at once the Mother Superior.

Toward eventide the longed for miracle happened, the boy monk awoke from sound slumber and turning his head slightly found a young acolyte girl asleep in a chair by the hearth nearby. First examining his immediate circumference- blanket and bindings and sore sewed forehead- he searched the room for his cloak and long gloves.

Within the cloak was the foretelling finger of his future, his fate. As Mother surmised from the lack of tonsure, the military-trained muscular body, and the body runes, he was not a boy monk. He was a young Wizard being transported, no doubt under stealthy guard, to serve some summoning high and lofty potentate of the land, or more likely to be tried by him. His kind came every five hundred years; the last had died sixteen years before, at the time of the great betrayal and invasion. The boy's very existence was unexpected, a mystery.

Attempting to sit up, the boy immediately felt a flush of face and dizzily reclined back into his pillow. He then called his sleeping keeper awake. M'Illie awoke with a start, stood up dizzying herself a bit, and forthwith headed for the door. The manly commanding voice arrested her and drew her back.

"Girl, where am I; where are my companions, and where is my cloak and gloves?" barked the boy monk in military-ordering baritone.

M'Illie froze, and turned to look at the now-awakened eyes. Like the rest of him, she found her charge's piercing blue eyes well-set, well-formed, and well, extremely fair. She swallowed in virgin-blushing silence. He turned his fair head a bit and fairly gazed at her as if fairly smitten. At least that is how she drank-in the gaze.

"My cloak?" whispered the boy, hoping his more-civil bark would cause his fearful keeper to, at the least, civilly obey.

"On yon chair, my lord," whispered M'Illie back.

"Fetch it for me?" petitioned the boy, prayerfully. M'Illie complied and fetched it.

"Cover me, will you?" begged the fair-haired one.

"Aye, my lord," acolyte responded with curtsy, and covered the boy as requested.

"From your habit I take it I am in a nunnery and you an acolyte of the Fair Savior's Lady?"

"Aye, my lord," M'Illie responded, again with curtsy, head bowed.

"I and my companions were caught unawares and attacked most viciously on the forest road by brigands most fierce and foul. Did any other survive? What of Father, the old man?" begged the boy in tender-tenor-tone with pools filling limpid eyes.

"None survived but you, my lord, and are now at rest beneath the sacred soil," M'Illie replied with bowed head. "You were brought to us wounded and in deep-fevered sleep by a logger and son. We feared you but an inch from death's open door ready to join your companions."

Fingering the left outer under-hem of the cloak with his right hand, the boy, with anxious relief found what he had been looking for. He breathed in, then out deeply, closing his eyes briefly in gratitude. Had only the robbers known the price for his ransom or the treasure he carried concealed in a seam!

M'Illie stepped closer and felt the boy's brow for fever. It had abated. Then for the first time in her life, she yielded to innocent temptation. She fingered some of the long flowing blonde locks back into place.

"God's thanks for all you've done for me. May I speak to your Mother Superior?" requested the boy monk.

"Aye, my lord; but what shall we call you. What is the name I shall give Mother to address you by?"

"Randy is my given name from birth."

"'Tis a strange, foreign name, is it not?"

"Aye it 'tis; when but a mere child of ten, I was taken by Vikings from my far fair land of Rodendale and brought to this, to Royaume'el. The brothers bought me from slavers, trained me, and upon my marked ascendency renamed me T'Olarf, an even stranger name of a stranger more ancient dialect.

"You may tell your Mother and mine that she may address me as, T'Olarf."

"Aye, my lord, 'tis strange to my tongue indeed; I shall now away and announce to my Mother, our Mother, that you are awake and well."

M'Illie turns to depart the room. T'Olarf forbids her.

"And how shall I call you, my fair savior?"

With a blush of rose, M'Illie turns her head slightly, tells her name and withdraws closing the door behind her. T'Olarf breathes in deeply and exhales loudly, locks both hands behind his head- uncautiously and uncaringly revealing sacred secret banned-upon-pain-of-death runic sign- smiles, and prays his hunger soon will be as satisfied as his vision.

****

After knocking at Mother Superior's privy chamber door, invited in M'Illie declared, "Dear Mother, the young master has awakened and asked for you."

"And did he speak to you other than asking to speak with me?" Mother Superior asked arising from prayer at privy sainted altar.

"Aye, Mother. He said to tell you that you may address him as T'Olarf- a name given him by brother monks upon his marked ascendency."

"It was not brother monks who named him, child. They were brother wizards. You are sure he called himself by the name T'Olarf?" Mother asked, clutching at prayer beads more tightly.

"Aye, my gracious Mother; a strange name is it not?"

"It is a name I have not heard for many years...and thought I'd never hear again. Sit child, I must to you make confession."

Mother took her seat near the warming hearth and beckoned her young suddenly doubting daughter in faith to take the seat nearest her.

"You will hear the tale soon enough from the young man's own lips. When I first gazed upon him, I was struck almost dumb at the likeness. Now, I know 'tis a true likeness to his late father, my late husband."

"You were once married, my Mother?"

"It was a long time ago, long before the graying head, before the great betrayal and invasion. The young man who stole this fishmonger daughter's heart was a young wizard, too. Fair of hair, skin, and countenance, he bore the same runic sign as the young man in the priest's house.

"He is my returned son."

"But Mother, how can you be sure of this?"

The Mother Superior pulled from beneath her habit a gold-chained locket inscribed with runic sign. She explained that, with the nuptial vows to her wizard, came a solemn more sacred obligation. The locket was her death.

"You see daughter, a wizard may marry. If he marry he may tell his wife the mysteries of the runic sign inscribed upon his body, but he may or may not reveal the magic of it. If captured and tortured, the wife must take her own life before revealing the secrets of the rune, how they are read, their interpretation, and their power.

"During the great invasion, I was captured whilst my beloved was attending our great king, O'Aedello. My husband's runes foretold him of my capture. He was by oath and obedience bound, by stealth of magic, to get the locket to me, so that I could drink the poison within. This is when the great betrayal happened.

"My T'Olarf was to aide me in my death. He then would use his runic magic, defeat the usurper king, Angstgutt, and send him and his kind back across the sea. Instead, he used his stealthy magic, rescued me, great with child; captured, he took his own life.

"That was the betrayal. My T'Olarf gave his life for me and our untimely born son at the cost of our king, his kindred, and kingdom.

"Once delivered, I gave my babe to my sister. She and her husband ferried him across the sea to Rodendale. Somehow, my son has returned and become his father. What could it all mean?"

M'Illie knelt before her Mother confessor and tried with hugs and heart to comfort her as she wept holding the deadly locket.

"Mother, take heart; your son has returned. Though I did not understand it at the time, I do now understand. Before I took my leave, he said, 'You may tell your mother and *mine*, that she may address me as, T'Olarf."

Upon the hearing of it, the Mother Superior pulled her daughter in faith into her bosom. Standing each dried the other's happy tears. Mother had more to reveal before she and the acolyte crossed the threshold of the priest's bedroom door.

"My child, my son has not returned for me. He has returned for thee. I cannot upon pain of death, reveal the secrets of the runic sign upon him. Only he can reveal that to his beloved.

"We shall attend him shortly, and I shall tend my motherly welcome and farewell."

"But my vows; the order," M'Illie protested as they left privy chamber.

"Your fair hair has not yet been sheared, as the hairs of this graying head many years ago. You are but acolyte and not yet nun.

"You are free to follow your heart. You are free, my daughter, to marry," encouraged the Mother Superior.

"But I do not know my heart, Mother. How can I reject marriage to the King of the Universe even for a wizard? How do I know that I shall not refuse death if called upon to betray my beloved?" M'Illie protested.

"My son, your lord, will soon reveal all to you, my daughter. Be comforted by my counsel and his love. Now, we must away and attend my son."

* * * * * * * * * * *

Upon crossing bedroom threshold, mother and daughter found son in bed with cloak pulled up over shoulders, arms under cover. T'Olarf smiled upon seeing his true mother and true wife. He withdrew his runed arms and beckoned them near. He first kissed his mother on cheeks and lips and the pair wept hard into each other. M'Illie wept too at seeing the joy.

Not saying a word, Mother took daughter's right hand and placed it into her son's left hand. She then took her silent thankful leave. M'Illie turned and briefly nodded her goodbye. Mother closed the door.

"May I speak, my gracious lord?" M'Illie importuned.

"Surely, after you've summoned me supper, my gracious but forgetful wife," T'Olarf ordered with a mischievous wink and grin.

"Oh my heavens, I had not considered. You must be well-starved. Forgive me my lord."

M'Illie, light and fair of foot, ran to catch Mother up. After relaying hospitable request, she quickly returned to her beloved.

"Forgive me my lord," M'Illie begged, taking her seat by her beloved on the bed.

Something an acolyte of the order of the Fair Savior's Lady would surely never do.

"In truth, I am starved to an inch from death's open door. Only love can now save me."

T'Olarf's countenance feigning faint at the first, soon became the devil's own grin. Taking M'Illie's hand again, he beckoned her to scoot closer to him. Blushing her reply, she scooted closer.

"Before food and love's talk I must impart to you, upon pain of your death, the meaning of my runes. In Wizard-speak, it is a sort of proposal of marriage, if thou wouldst take it so; and so you may take *some* comfort in that."

M'Illie smiled, laughed, and squeezed her espousal's hand. He smiled too, and then with grave countenance began to disclose the meaning of his body's runes.

"Here on my left underhand and arm is the past inscribed by magic rune. Across my shoulders and chest is the very present as we live and breathe. My right arm and hand are the mysteries of the future yet unveiled to man. That is not the magic of it, nor its true power.

"Fetch me a sharp knife, wife," T'Olarf commanded. M'Illie obeyed and fetched a knife most sharp from the eating table in an antechamber in the outer room.

Taking the knife in hand T'Olarf cut the inside seam behind the embroidery of the outer hem of his cloak. He pulled from it a wand made from the Red Ash tree, a most rare tree indeed, even in Royaume'el.

Touching a runic sign on his upper left underarm with the tip of the wand, a great ghostly scroll suddenly appeared before them. It unrolled revealing a story in runic-rhyming verse.

"This is the magic of reading the runic inscribed upon my body. Each sign is a single scroll or many. When a wizard takes his own wand and touches a sign, the true tale of that time- past, present, or future- is unveiled. Only he can read and interpret it.

"M'Illie, you can see why a tyrant king would torture and kill for a treasure such as this. With this knowledge, he would be a god. That, and love for my fair mother, is why my father took his own life and doomed a king and kingdom, sparing my mother and me.

"There was not to be another like T'Olarf the Elder for another five hundred years. Yet here am I, born late, and before my time to right the betrayal's wrongs, to avenge my father, and to win back the Kingdom of Royaume'el. This is what the runic scroll reads just here."

With a wave of the wand, the scroll disappeared as quickly as it had manifested. T'Olarf took the wand and touched a rune just below his left shoulder.

"Here M'Illie is the story of my birth; of my ferrying away, of my mother-aunt raising me. Here is my kidnapping by Vikings at the age of ten, of my two years of shame and sadness with them, of their selling me to slavers. Just here, the slavers sell me to my spiritual father, the old man who now lies beneath the sacred soil.

"The men you and E'Rik the elder and younger assumed were brother's mine, traveling companions, were not.

"They were sent by the tyrant usurper king to arrest me and take me and my Father for trial in the capital city, Esparusia. It also tells of the attack and murder of all but me."

"My lord, you knew all this would come to pass?"

"I knew not that my mother was my aunt. I knew none of this until after the sacred runes were inscribed upon my body, until I knew the power of the runic wand of the Red Ash tree.

"The inscribing was painful and lasted three years, until I was presented the wand and ascended to my marked calling.

"But yes, once the future had moved to the near present, I was able to read the signs. Then I sewed up my wand to protect it, as is my poisoned locket necklace sewed within my cloak."

With another wave of the wand, the runic scroll disappeared as quickly as it had manifested. T'Olarf then pulled down his cloak further revealing his broad manly runic chest.

"See here, M'Illie this is you. Just above my heart, here. This is our story, as we live it and breathe it now." T'Olarf touched the sign with tip of wand and another scroll manifested in ghostly fashion before them.

"So that is how our Mother knew who you were and what you were at the first," M'Illie surmised.

"Yes. I am sure she doubted upon seeing me. When she saw that I wore no monk's tonsure upon my head, and the sacred runes, and the fashion of their inscribing upon my body, it led her to finger the hem of my cloak to reveal its hidden treasure. She knew me from the first."

"And now I know you, my beloved."

M'Illie leaned forward causing wizard to drop his wand. Ancient secret runic scroll evaporated but they took no notice. T'Olarf invited his foretold love into his runic embrace; she was his past, present, and future now, and he hers. With the deepest kiss of love's magic, the boy Wizard began the consummation of their love, and gently abed took M'Illie as his wife.

M'Illie, at once, found herself in deepest love and quickly unqualified to be a nun of the Fair Savior's Lady. Thankfully, the banquet was shortly thereafter delivered by a host of blushing acolytes and a very happy mother. After all, the food and drink was not just to prevent the boy wizard- surely an inch from death's open door- from famished faint. T'Olarf needed to replenish his waning sorely tested strength for that which in runic rhyme of old, now in common tongue foretold...

> *For seven days hence the runic signs were read,*
> *For seven days and nights the couple was abed.*
> *In nature's appointed time, a child was born,*
> *The land of Royaume'el delivered*
> *By saving Wizard's horn.*

Alexander and Hephaiston

"Are you going to spot me or just stand there?"

"I'm admiring the view."

(Herbert walks over and spots Gabriel.)

"You've never seen a guy do reps before?"

"Not as handsome as you."

"You really are sure of yourself. I hope those freckles on your arms and hands don't wear off, or slide off your nose when you sweat."

(Gabriel continues his reps. Herbert giggles.)

"They're not freckles."

"What are they, then?"

"Love spots. I'm going to make love to you for every one of them."

(Herbert holds down the bar bell forcing Gabriel to look squarely into his upside down blue eyes.)

"I think I'm going to make you one of my girls. I need a redhead."

(Gabriel forces the bar up with a grunt.)

"I think you're going to make me *your* girl. How much is your max?"

(Herbert presses down on the bar again, frustrating Gabriel just a little more. He becomes red-faced.)

"I can surely bench press your mother-fucking ass.

"What are you, a buck eighty-five soaking wet?"

"A buck seventy-five. And honey, you can bench press me all night long."

(Gabriel replaces the bar, sits up, stands and turns around facing his flirty spotter.)

"You got a name, fish?"

"Wow, fish. I hope you're more original in bed. I haven't been called a fish for quite a while. I've just arrived from gladiator camp."

"Been there, done that. You got a name, fish?"

"Herbert, but you may call me Herb?"

"Weed, you want me to call you weed?"

"No. Let's call *you* 'weed' so I can smoke you all night long."

"My name's Gabriel, at least on the yard. I'm in six-house."

"So am I."

Gabriel dries the sweat from his forehead and neck with a towel showing off his fully loaded *guns*. He leads his new acquaintance out of the gym and onto the prison yard for a more private conversation. They walk the track toward six-house.

"You're kinda cute. I think I may just keep you for myself. What do we do when we run out of freckles?"

"By then, I'll have age spots, and you can start counting them for every...slow...fuck."

"I don't like my new cellie. I'll have him moved out and you moved in tomorrow."

"You can pull strings like that?"

"Let's just say that I'd have you in my cell tonight if it wasn't for the red tape. But... yeah, you'll move in tomorrow after lunch."

"You said you go by 'Gabriel' on the yard. What do I call you in private?"

"You may call me Alexander; I'm full-blood Greek."

"Like Alexander the Great?"

"You know a little history. Maybe you have a little Greek in you."

"No. I'm German-Irish. But I'd love to have a little Greek in me...or a lot of Greek."

"That can be arranged."

"If you're Alexander, does that make me Hephaiston?"

"Wow...yeah...You are Hephaiston, but I'll call you Herbie."

****

Entering six-house, Gabriel turns to go into his wing. Herbie whispers something into Gabriel's ear before he walks to the door leading into his wing.

"I can't wait for the honeymoon."

As the lock of his wing's door pops, Gabriel gives Herbie a serious glance and asks, "Hey, you got a head for business?" Herbie winks his reply.

It was not something Gabriel had expected while incarcerated. He had not only fallen in love, but he had fallen in love at first sight with a freckly-faced man about his age but a good four inches taller. There was an immediate chemistry that he had never experienced with another human being- male or female.

As he lay on his top bunk, he allowed himself, for the first time in many years, the luxury to feel human. Thinking about Herbie, Gabriel tingled from head to toe. He breathed in love's intoxicating air and refused to exhale. Then 'the thoughts' came.

'Is this love or am I just wanting it to be? Maybe my feelings are just my subconscious trying to cope with my aloneness and loneliness.' Gabriel then answered those philosophic thoughts with, 'Would I be having these doubts if there wasn't something *real* to doubt about?'

The thing that most disturbed Gabriel was not the doubts. It was that he was second-guessing himself. Since he had worked and fought hard to carve out his position on the yard and in his housing unit, he had never second-guessed himself. Right or wrong, he was always decisive. He had to be, or men would see it and take it as weakness.

Then reality hit Gabriel like a ton of bricks. As soon as he had 'invited' Herbie to spot him, he had violated his own rules. He had acted 'human' even flirty in the presence of other inmates. Had Herbie revealed a weakness or made him weak? Could he risk being weak- even around Herbie? Was being in love worth the risk of losing his position and power on the yard?

Then another reality hit him. He had known guys 'like' Herbie for years- players, manipulators, free-loaders, hoping to quickly insinuate themselves into an association with a powerbroker on the yard for their own protection. Had he been duped and played by this fish? If he had, then Herbie was one of the best players he had ever met and surely would make a great storeman in his housing unit. That alone would make him an asset as a cellie.

"Yeah, he'd make a great storeman for me," Gabriel whispered, reassuring himself of his first impression of the man.

Gabriel felt he was in control again. He would take whatever motivated Herbie to insinuate himself into an association with him and use him as he had used so many other young men who tried to play him. Then something 'middle school' happened.

Lying there worrying about not showing weakness and projecting power, as he tried to map out how he was going to use Herbie, Gabriel got an erection- and not just any old erection. It was the boner of all boners. Even thinking that Herbie was trying to play him, he found himself attracted to him and horny as hell.

"Shit. I can't even think about freckle-boy without getting a boner.

"Well, he looks like he'd be good for a fuck anyway- more than I'll be getting from my new cellie," Gabriel whispered to himself.

Rolling onto his side, Gabriel looked down at his old geezer of a cellie, who had arrived that morning on the same bus as Herbie, and informed him to pack his shit, that he was moving out the next day. He then rolled onto his stomach, pressed his hard manmeat into the mattress, clenched his butt cheeks, released, and dreamed of his handsome freckly-faced player, soon to be storeman.

Herbert congratulated himself as he lay on the top bunk of his now 'temporary' cell. Within a few hours of his arrival at FCC, he had found out who the powerbrokers were, had located one- a handsome muscular Greek pimp- had played him like a fiddle, and was now under his protection and would soon be his cellie and lover.

"Not bad for a few hours' work," Herbert remarked.

He'd had worse- way worse. Herbert was grateful that his new protector was young, handsome, and a power to be reckoned with on the yard. It was serendipitous- a stroke of luck, really- that his new cellie's name was Alexander and that he too was a 'fan' of the great man and had studied the history. He had from his mouth- the lingering tingling effect left the man deaf, blind, dumb and paralyzed. If the strong supporting arms withdrew, he would surely collapse and melt into the floor.

He was, in a word, *goo*. Standing there unable to ask for more, Herbie was awakened by a light slap to the face. When he opened his eyes, he found olive green eyes staring questioningly at him.

"Are you going to be my storeman, or not?"

Herbie nodded. He could not speak. Every molecule of his mouth tingled along with the rest of him. He stared in amazement at the man before him wondering if any human being had ever been kissed like that before. He surely hadn't. The player could not breathe and with no oxygen left in his brain, he could not think. If he couldn't think, then he couldn't scheme- plan his next move.

Gabriel studied his new cellie a few seconds then leaned in closer. The minty breathe was warm to Herbie's cheek. He felt his knees going again. Just the anticipation of the man caused him to swoon and almost faint. Strong arms again took him pulling off his shirt.

Greek fire again launched from Trireme-tongue striking neck and nipples, then penetrated heart and soul. The fire engulfed Herbie, left him adrift- rudderless, at the mercy of the maker of it. Again, he surrendered but this time sank to the floor unable to take the weight of it upon his long-developed, now shattered emotional defenses.

Alexander had disarmed and overpowered his Hephaiston. He knelt by him on the floor and continued his tongue attack. Deeper it went into the throat until it eventually slowed Hephaiston's fast-beating heart. He could happily die now. He had tasted- no, had been consumed by...love and felt whole, complete, at peace.

In one motion, with lips still locked in love's devotion,
Alexander lifted Hephaiston from floor to bed.
With deepest affection's tenderest of kisses,
Lover was undressed ne'er a word was said.

The conqueror shed his clothes; the world did not exist.
No privacy was thought of or modesty missed.
Alexander conquered his Hephaiston
With a kiss!

From that day on, lasting several years, the pair was inseparable. On the yard they played handball, one-on-one basketball, baseball, and jogged together. In the gym they were each other's spotters, boxing partners, and volleyball team mates. They ate together, read together, and worked together, slept for a few hours each night, together. They were truly one.

Their relationship and daily routine could be described in two words: cuddling and dancing. When cuddling, Herbie, the taller of the two, would have Gabriel recline into him and hold him as they read a book or watched TV from the bottom bunk. When not cuddling, they would slow dance to music on the radio/cassette player or to one or the other singing into an ear.

Once-in-a-while, they would wrestle, as young men living in close quarters tend to do- Herbie trying to pin the quicker stronger Gabriel. Nevertheless, he loved being pinned by Gabriel. That was always the point and the end of their wrestling matches.

There was only one brief hiccup in their relationship. After a year of cohabitation, Herbie begged Gabriel to perform anal sex on him. Up until that time, remembering his gang rapes at The Walls, Gabriel had allowed Herbie this intimacy, but refused to perform the same intimacy on Herbie. Gabriel finally agreed to take a blood test at the infirmary to determine finally if he was HIV positive or not. Herbie took the test, too.

For two weeks, the men waited. It was torture. It was the unseen elephant in the room. They cuddled and danced, but did not talk much during that fortnight of foreboding.

When Gabriel got his results, the powerbroker, the conqueror was conquered. He stripped himself naked like a King David mourning the death of his young son, beautiful Absalom, weeping inconsolably into his pillow. Herbie climbed atop the bunk bed, and held him from behind and wept hard into him, soaking his back and his mother. No words violated the sacredness of the mourning moment.

Suddenly, with the strength of love's resolve, Gabriel awoke from his slumber of sadness. Herbie's test came back negative. He would not allow him to get the plague. He feared that even his kisses might one day infect him. He also did not want Herbie nearby when he got full-blown AIDS. He must be sent away.

Gabriel, for the most part, had ended his career as a prostitute after Herbie arrived. He continued giving 'head' for the right price, but was not a 'full-service' girl. He arranged for his other girls to do those jobs. From the day Herbie arrived, Gabriel stopped dressing in drag, at least on the yard. When diagnosed with HIV, he ended all of his 'extracurricular' activities on the yard and with Herbie, as well. This was just after their fortnight of foreboding.

For the next fortnight the two argued, threw cups and clothes and sneakers at each other, but their arguments always ended in a cuddle. After all, who else could better comfort them in their distress? Their dream of a 'happily-ever-after' was now a shared nightmare.

There was only one way out of their nightmare. Gabriel begged Herbie to move out, to find a new cellie and lover. Herbie believed the remedy was for them to become even more 'one'. In Gabriel's mind, that option was unthinkable and impossible. Then 'that night' came.

"Herbie, stop it! For fuck's sake, stop it!"

Herbie continued.

"If you don't stop, I swear to God I'm going to beat you senseless and bloody, and you know I can and will."

Silence continued with the 'oral'.

"Goddamnit, I said stop!"

Gabriel readies himself to strike Herbie hard on the side of the head, but then checks himself. If he strikes him too hard, Herbie's teeth might tear the skin of his penis. He might bleed into his mouth. He would end up doing what he was trying to prevent. Gabriel begins to weep.

Without a word, Herbie stops, looks lovingly up at his lover, drops to his lower berth and assumes the position. Taking a moment to wipe his eyes, Gabriel looks down at his naked cellie on knees with torso lying on his mattress. He knew what he wanted…it wasn't sex.

Gabriel jumped to the floor and looked out the door portal for any CO that might be lurking about. He longs to embrace his lover and to kiss him, but he does not. He studies him in the shadows of his cell and soul. Reverently bowing his head, he pulls down his boxers and kneels behind him.

Weeping, Gabriel jacks-off trying to get it hard again. He cannot. He weeps harder and hugs his lover from behind, soaking his freckled back. Hephaiston does not look back. It is almost as if he has fallen asleep, but he is wide-awake. He longs for and braces for the penetrating 'kisses' of his *Alexander*.

By force of will or force of love- he does not know which- Alexander, about to drool spit onto his almost hard member, discovers the petroleum jelly with his fingers. He surrenders and sexes his cellie.

At the moment of sad unsweet release, Gabriel purposes to withdraw. He cannot poison *his* Herbie. As he tries to pull out, long freckled arms reach back and freckled hands pull him in again. It is fated. *Hephaiston* will die with his *Alexander*.

****

For the next several years, Gabriel and Herbie made love unrestrained. They were one in every sense of the word- in shared trial, in shared treatment, in shared trust.

Eventually, Herbie got his walking papers from the parole board. Prior to his release his mother had written that she and his father couldn't accept a son who had turned homosexual. Herbie moved in with Gabriel's mother and grandmother. They loved him as they loved Gabriel. Herbie said as much during phone calls and in letters. Alexander never took another lover and became withdrawn, sullen, and deeply unhappy. He started appearing on the yard again in drag.

Within a year of Herbie's release, having walked down two-thirds of his time, and factoring in good behavior and the disease that he carried, the parole board released Gabriel. He and Herbie lived a short time with mama and grandma. When yiayia died, she left Gabriel a small fortune. Mama sold the family businesses and the family home at that time.

Not long after those events, family, friends, and a few former inmate acquaintances got post cards that read as follows:

Alexandros, Hephaiston, and Mama are leaving the U.S.A. forever and will henceforth reside in 'The Land of beginning again'

In my mind, the 'Land of beginning again' could only mean one place. To this day, I see Alexandros and Hephaiston lying on an Aegean beach with Mama in the white kitchen of a white villa just up the rocky hill preparing their wonderful lunch of lamb and fresh garden vegetables. (With the new advances and drug treatments, I expect that the boys will, by destined-fate and despite their fatal disease, live long lives.)

Did the freckles ever wear off? I believe some surely did. Nevertheless, I also believe that Gabriel will count each and every one of them. When they run out, he will start counting age spots.

Esmeralda and Quasimodo, the Hunchback Telemarketeer: A Fairy Tale

"My name is Quasimodo, and I am a Telemarketeer.

"Why am I a Telemarketeer? It's because I am so ugly.

"Besides that, I am a Hunchback.

"What you mean?

"Of course I have had 'real' jobs before.

"I've been a used car salesman...for a day.

"I've even worked at a nursery selling flowers and potted plants.

"But children seem to recoil and flee at my grotesque presence, and then they return to throw rotten fruit and vegetables at me.

"I do like the overripe bananas, I must confess.

"Once, I heard a priest say in the very shadow of Notre Dame Cathedral that every man is born with a divine spark; that we are all born in the grace of God.

"But I've often wondered if some might not have fallen a bit from it.

"And after meeting a few used car salesmen, I've wondered if some haven't fallen right out of it."

Quasimodo laughs hard causing something unplanned and unexpected to happen. The room erupts in laughter. The Hunchback blushes shame.

"No need to blush my good Quasi. It was a fine respectable fart needing no introduction. It should be bottled and sold. It came with credentials and needs no resume," Esmeralda rescued, leaning over from her cubicle, laughing.

The floor manager was neither pleased nor amused. As he approached the offender's cubicle...the resume did come. Quasimodo, wearing a mischievous grin, let go a little toot or a poot.

"Quasimodo! How many times have I directed you to the toilet to take care of your hygienic problems? How many times have I told you- it is *telemarketer* not *telemarketeer*? And how many times have I instructed you not to tell your pitiful life story to the customers? You are to prompt them into setting appointments for our salesmen. You are here to sell them on setting window and siding appointments!"

"Could you hold please? Thanks ever so much.

"Boss, it was the onions I ate at lunch, and I was trying to set an appointment. The customer asked *why* I didn't have a *real* job. I was just answering him honestly," Quasimodo explained, after putting his customer on hold.

"Besides, I want to be like my four friends who are true Musketeers, protectors of the King."

"*Mon Dieu*; do you know what you are? You are an imbecile! You are incapable of any meaningful employment. You are fired! You can now be a telemarketeer, as you call yourself, but you are no longer a telemarketer. Now, get out," declared the boss, pointing toward the door of the call center.

"You shouldn't take the Lord's name in vain, sir. It won't go well for you on the Day of Judgment. So says Archdeacon Frollo," Quasimodo whispered, gathering his few belongings to depart.

"Get Out!"

"Quasimodo is right, sir. You are doing a horrible thing. You should not dismiss a man with such flimsy cause, and you shouldn't use the name of the Lord in vain, especially on the call center floor in the hearing of callers and customers," rebuked the fair recently hired Esmeralda, coming to her co-workers defense.

"And it is right to fart on the floor? Are you also a telemarketeer? Has this room gone completely mental? Get out! See how you can earn a living wage on the streets," declared the boss, firing Esmeralda, as well.

"But sir, how shall I survive in this economy? No one is hiring. You leave us only the mercy of God to depend on," Esmeralda begged, clutching her bosses forearm.

"Perhaps you and I could go into my office and come to a mutual agreement, my dear? You are a beauty, though you defend this beast, and need not lose your job," the boss tempted, peering at ample bosom, grabbing Esmeralda's naked knee.

"I'd rather die a street-walker than submit to you, pig. Come Quasi and introduce me to your friends."

Esmeralda shook off her now red-faced boss's advances and left arm-n-arm with her smiling still-farting Hunchback friend.

****

While walking along *Rue de la Seconde Chance*, near *Boulevard St. Jude*, the patron saint of hopeless causes, Quasimodo and Esmeralda are almost run over by four fleeing fugitives. Upon looking back and around, feeling safe, they pause to shake the hand of their recognized friend and his lady fair.

"My noble lady, may I introduce to you my brothers bearing no arms. These are my friends, the Musketeers- Athos, Porthos, Aramis, and their new friend and defender of the faith, the recently arrived to Paris and to be knighted, the youth, d'Artagnan," Quasimodo proudly declared.

"Gentleman," Esmeralda greeted with blushing extended hand. Each man rushed to kiss the ungloved hand...several times- all but the youth, d'Artagnan.

"Boys, if the lady wanted a bath, she would away to her apartments," Quasimodo prevented, stepping forward to shoo his amorous friends back and aside.

"But I have no apartment, Quasi. I am recently evicted. Where do you and your friends reside?" Esmeralda inquired, giggling.

"These are urchins of the street, my lady. I reside above the rafters of Notre Dame. I call it home, though it is far from a house. You may share my humble quarters, if you will," Quasimodo offered, blushing.

"For now, it may be best. I trust we may supper with your friends, anon?" asked Esmeralda to the delight of her new devotees.

"We dine at six my lady in Cathedral Baptistery's shadow. But first there is the stealing..." Athos proffered, but was quickly interrupted by Porthos.

"*Shopping*, we have shopping to do, my fair one."

"Until then," Aramis interjected, insinuating another kiss on the hand; the handsome d'Artagnan stood by in boyish-blushing silence worshipping from afar.

"Until then," Quasimodo agreed. Taking Esmeralda in arm, he led her to Cathedral Notre Dame.

****

"My Father Frollo, may I introduce to you my new friend, Esmeralda. She recently has no job, money, or place to live. May she for a time share my modest dwelling?" Quasimodo begs his surrogate father and caretaker.

At first Frollo, caught unawares, is disarmed by the beauty before him. His chaste heart and celibate body suddenly consumed with the flames of sexual desire, and he finds, to his dismay, no desire within him to put them out.

"Your name, my child," Father Frollo asks.

"I am called Esmeralda, your grace."

"Such vulgar accommodations are unseemly for a creature of such beauty. It would also be unseemly for you to share my apartments. However, I could allow you the spare room reserved for visiting clergy. It is near my apartments," Father Frollo offered, clutching his gold crucifix.

"It would be no trouble for you?" Esmeralda asks.

"Quasimodo, are you prepared to ring the evening bells? It is almost six O'clock. I will show the fair Esmeralda her room," Father Frollo directed.

Quasimodo bowed in humble obedience and retreated to ring the great cathedral bells. Afterward, he would escort Esmeralda outside for supper with the Musketeers.

After showing the sleeping room with no bathroom, the archdeacon offered his new tenant the use of his bathroom. He then offered to share his sumptuous supper. At first Esmeralda refused, but then yielded upon hearing the menu. She had rarely eaten such fine fare. Forgetting disfigured Quasimodo and his poor but handsome friends, she withdrew and bathed in the archdeacon's bath while he waited outside longing to embrace her.

When Quasimodo returned to fetch Esmeralda, Father Frollo forbad entrance to his apartment, stated that the lady was indisposed unable to join him and his friends. He shut the door upon the forlorn fellow and Quasimodo withdrew to attend his friends outside.

"Where's the lady fair?" asked d'Artagnan.

"She is tired and abed. So said the priest, my Father," Quasimodo answered.

"She'll be more tired without supper," Porthos counseled.

"Look what we pilfered for her;" offered Aramis, "here is a roasted chicken, fresh roasted carrots, bread, and wine. Who could offer better fare for the fair?"

"She's probably dining with the priest," bemoaned young uninhibited d'Artagnan.

"Why would you say such a thing? He has been as dear as a father to me. He would not deceive me so. He offered Esmeralda a far finer apartment than I could. She simply went to bed," Quasimodo defended.

"Yes, a bath and then abed...with the priest," Aramis advised.

"Slanderer; you take that back! Esmeralda may be a Gipsy, but she is a nice girl. Frollo is a priest, consecrated. He would never," Quasimodo declared, defending his love and his father-friend.

"Come; let us eat while the food is still warm and undiscovered. Stolen meats are sweet, they say. This bickering accomplishes nothing," Athos recommended in goodly counsel.

With regret of their missing quest, each man crossed his thanks to God for food and drink and ate heartily. The urchins of the street soon returned to their beds in the

Cirque de fous. Quasimodo retreated into the cathedral and for a time took his watch in the shadows outside the archdeacon's apartments.

About ten O'clock anxious fears were confirmed when Esmeralda exited to return to her sleeping room. Disrobed smiling priest waved his farewell and closed his door. Quasimodo quickly pursued his faithless friend.

"You slept with Frollo?" sadly accused Quasimodo.

"Quasimodo," answered the girl in a start.

"Frollo offered a bath and a banquet and a bed. He is a priest. How could I know he would force himself upon me? You should have warned me," Esmeralda confessed and accused, stopping at her sleeping room door.

Quasimodo looked at the torn sleeve of Esmeralda's dress and knew that she spoke the truth. The priest had tempted with bath, banquet, and bed, forcing himself upon her. Quasimodo withdrew to his bell tower in adopted shame. She withdrew to her bed and locked the door.

****

The bells of Notre Dame rang out shattering the still night calling the city awake to witness the crime of *that priest*. Quasimodo at first rode the great bells then descended and pulled the ropes again and again ringing the city to come and quench the fires consuming the hearts of two men- one, a lust-filled priest, the second, suffering from the fires of outrage.

The Musketeers were the first to arrive and quickly pulled the Hunchback off the ropes and restrained him. Archdeacon Frollo then arrived in panic to ask why the bells were ringing at such an ungodly hour, asking where the fire was. Esmeralda came too. She knew why

Quasimodo rang the bells; she knew what fires were ablaze in the great cathedral that hour of the night.

"You, you fornicator, you pig, Frollo! How could you spoil the fair Esmeralda?" Quasimodo accused.

At the hearing of the accusation, Frollo left for his apartments in an angry hurry. He soon returned with a great belt and began whipping Quasimodo just as his friends released him. The buckle tore eyelid and cheek, lips and ears, before the Musketeers grabbed the errant naïve of a priest and whipped him with the same back shameless to his apartments. Esmeralda could do naught but weep in the shadowed corner near pillared-saint.

The first to reach Esmeralda for comfort was d'Artagnan. He gentlemanly lifted the lady up and escorted her out the great front doors to the great front steps. It was there that he met the whole district ready to douse a fire. Aramis quickly arrived thereafter and beckoned the crowd to disperse.

"Some crazed lunatic rang the bells, but he has been arrested. Go home, rest, good people. There is no fire...now."

Porthos and Athos assisted Quasimodo up to his dwelling place. There they tended his wounds, offered the wine that would have been their breakfast, and left him to a restless sleep. They then joined their companions and escorted Esmeralda to their dwelling beneath some obscure stairwell in the *Cirque de fous*. Guarded, she feared no more molesting or disturbance for the remainder of the night.

At the cockcrow of morning, Quasimodo awakened with a start. He sorely got up and quickly descended to find his love gone, not in the sleeping room. Unaware that she had been safely spirited away by his friends, the street urchin Musketeers, he knocked loudly and disrespectfully at the apartment door of his former father-friend.

"Where is she? What have you done with her?" Quasimodo demanded, throttling the priest back into his apartment.

"She is not here. Look yourself; perhaps she took a taxi in the night. The whore is gone," Frollo bitterly protested.

Quasimodo searched the priest's apartments in a fretful fright and found them as he had said. He then ran out into the central nave and screamed his anguish to God in the hearing of the few faithful attending their souls in prayer. The priest shut his door to prepare his self and soul for daily service to God.

Retreating from his home, Notre Dame, Quasimodo ran as fast as his deformed body could manage to the *Cirque de fous*. There, to his great relief, he found her. There his angel was asleep on covers surrounded by his four friends. The Musketeers had done their job well. He turned aside to use a payphone nearby.

Within thirty minutes of the Telemarketeer's call, the police arrived at Cathedral Notre Dame and arrested priest adorned in holy vestments about to minister the body and blood of his once Lord. He had not yet made confession of his crime to his brother priest confessor and had not received absolution for his grievous sin. Saved that day from making himself a sacrilege-sinner, Frollo was taken away in handcuffs by civil ministering angels.

Later, the Telemarketeer and his Musketeer friends ate a hearty pilfered breakfast and wondered aloud what they were to do with the fair Esmeralda. Quasimodo knew in his heart that she could never love him as he was. So, he asked in the presence of fools and friends whom she would choose to be her protector...and lover.

To fool and friend's chagrin,
Esmeralda chose a boy as lover, not just friend.
As one, that wondrous sunlit day;
The pair walked arm-n-arm away.

Not halfway down the street,
Echoed loudly, d'Artagnan did repeat,
"Thou art a man, my blushing bride?
No matter, anon we celebrate in gayest pride."

Joey and Lucy, a love story made right

Blue is the sky
 Green is the trees
The majesty of birdsong
 Drives me to my knees

For the first time in many years, Joey breathed in freedom's crisp pungent air. The sky was cloudless and a deep blue. The pine trees a few yards from the gate of his release were loaded with cones. It was the greenest green and the bluest blue he had ever seen.

"My brother," Fred greeted, walking up and bear hugging Joey.

"My man," Joey answered patting Fred on the back.

"Honey-bee, you're lookin' good. I'm hungry for your nectar, but I expect I'll need to strap on a two-by-four after big ole' Freddie's fifteen years of service to ya," Joey greeted, laughing.

Lucy walked from the truck, handed Joey his leather jacket with the club's emblem emblazoned on the back, and kissed him deeply. "Daddy-bee, you know that ain't true," Lucy responded. The 5' 10" Joey boxed Fred's ribs playfully, admiringly sizing-up the 6'3" frame.

Fred laughed, then shoulder-hugged his best friend.

"Lucy may need a two-by-four to drive you out of her snatch-patch, that's for sure."

Fred laughed heartily again. The approaching suddenly blushing couple heard the repartee and tried to feign deafness.

"Hello dad," greeted the squirt. Thomas, now twenty-one, the spit-n-image of his dad, with his entwined girlfriend Anna, received welcomed hugs and cheek kisses.

"So it's off to Colorado? Can't you guys wait a day or two?" Joey asked, as he walked arm-n-arm with Lucy in the direction of Fred's pickup and the rental truck parked in the prison parking lot.

"This is your second honeymoon, man. The squirt and me and Anna will get your cabin set up in Colorado. We'll see you there in two or three days," announced Fred, kissing Lucy goodbye on the cheek, then shaking Joey's hand.

Behind the truck was parked Joey's Chopper with two helmets sitting on the seat. Thomas and Anna hopped in the rental, started the engine and waved goodbye. Fred hopped in his loaded tarped pickup with his chopper on a trailer in tow and did the same. The surrogate husband-father and his surrogate son and girlfriend were off to their club and home in the Rocky Mountains.

Joey and Lucy donned their helmets and mounted the Chopper. After Lucy handed her husband of twenty years a pair of round dark sunglasses, he revved the engine and headed for a threshold that he had never seen or crossed in his life- Lucy and Fred's home near the prison.

Arriving at the now all but empty house, upon their dismounting the purring beast, the couple shed their helmets and sunglasses. Joey swept Lucy off her feet and carried her over the threshold, closed and locked the door. The kiss came just as quickly. In that instant, the man exchanged his tortuous self-imposed prison celibacy for that of most satisfying erotic love.

Letting his wife down, Joey tore the blouse and jeans then the shoes right off of her. Before dropping to his knees, he paused only to delight in discovering that Lucy wore no bra or panties. He threw her left leg over his right shoulder. She yielded with a sigh and a shutter to the teasing tongue suddenly imposed upon her clitoris and the rough muscular hands rubbing and pinching at her hard nipples. Harley hubby was home and feasting like the starved man that he was.

Returning to full rosy lips, Joey shared the nectar he had harvested from Lucy's moist loins. He withdrew his tongue only to look and marvel at her teeth. The meth-damaged-beyond-repair teeth removed and replaced with a set of splendid, beautiful, perfectly white teeth- the kind he had foolishly tried to get for her by muling drugs- another gift from Fred. That was past. Husband was home with his one and only love.

At the pause, Lucy unsnapped her husband's blue jean shirt revealing a once boyish-trim, now muscular manly torso sporting rock-hard abs. As she dropped down, the jeans followed her. Joey kicked off his shoes quickly. No sooner than his jeans had dropped, he found his abs licked and his member caressed and kissed hard. Holding his wife's head gently at first, then more firmly, the man yielded in boyish delight to his first blowjob in over fifteen years.

Like a fifteen-year-old, not able to contain his joy or juices, Joey quickly drew his wife back into his arms, kissed her powerfully on the lips, and swept her off her feet again. He carried her down the hall of the small two-bedroom house, wondering where the bathroom was. Lucy directed to the second door on the right.

There, Joey found the shower stall as his partner had described it upon his last prison visit. Fred had removed the old green and pink tile and tub- from the sixties, no doubt- and replaced all with a tiled two-man shower stall. Still in socks, Joey opened the clear shower door and deposited Lucy within.

Giggling at the still-socked feet, Lucy knelt to remove them. Joey gladly yielded them up and out of the shower stall. But his wife's business wasn't done. Again, she caressed and kissed his member hard. Again, he almost lost his juices and lifted her up. Again, he went down upon her lifting both legs this time over his tanned muscular shoulders. Lucy leaned back in deepest conjugal pleasure and turned the shower dial until warm waters rained upon their still-youthful bodies.

Letting Lucy down and ascending again, Joey embraced his wife from behind and kissed her perfumed neck, nibbled at her ear lobes, all the while reaching his long toned deeply tanned arms and muscular hands to find the clitoris again. He fingered and stroked as he moved Lucy around and tongued her wet and glistening breasts. She kissed his head and neck and nibbled at his ear lobes when within reach.

Lifting his love, Joey implanted his throbbing hard manhood into her as she locked legs behind the back of his upper thighs. Holding wife firmly in grasp and against tiled wall, husband thrust and thrust repeatedly as she let go groans of absolute ecstasy. When the final release of long-imprisoned seed came- like their, at first fast-beating hearts, now slowed- it was orgasms in concert with a stereo of gasps and groans. It was hearts ever beating as one. An expression of life-long lovers truly designed, cupid-destined to be the completion of each other.

The orgasms calmed by deep kissing and a long embrace; then followed gentle hugs and kisses upon cheeks and necks. Tears followed; the lovers shampooed each other's long blonde flowing locks and sponged clean each other's bodies.

Upon opening the shower door, the couple found no towels either hanging or in the small closet. Smiling, Lucy took Joey's hand and led him dripping to the carpeted master bedroom a few feet away. There he spied sleeping bags side-by-side with a cassette player/radio and flashlights nearby. Beyond them were four white Turkish towels laying side by side lengthwise on the carpeted floor.

Wife invited husband upon the towels and in his embrace rolled upon and in them until their bodies were dry. Lucy then took smaller towels and dried her husband's hair and he returned the favor. She then led him down the hall to the empty dining room just off the empty living room.

"The electricity will be turned off by five this afternoon. That's why the flashlights. I have cold beer and bags of ice in the large cooler. There are T-bone steaks to grill. The pit is full of charcoal and ready to go. I have baked potatoes and corn on the cob ready to grill, too. There's also salad in the refrigerator," Lucy revealed.

"I'll slip on my jeans and get to grilling then," Joey responded, kissing his love on the cheek.

He was hungry...for food, now. Their first second honeymoon meal came with wine, dusk and candlelight sitting on the dining room floor. When they had their fill, Joey returned to the spot in the living room where he lost his shirt and had dismissed his vow of prison celibacy, reached into his pocket and retrieved a cassette tape.

Leading Lucy to the bedroom, Joey placed the cassette into the player and pulled off his jeans. To Lucy's delight and amusement, he played air guitar, rather provocatively, and sang beautifully and in key to Bryan Adam's song, *'Please forgive me'*. When the song was over and other equally powerful Bryan Adams love songs followed, Joey pulled his wife onto the sleeping bags. With both kneeling, he kissed deeply holding shoulders as Lucy grasped his rock-hard buttocks.

You are fair my love
My dove, my darling;
An angel from above,
You cause my heart to sing.

Moving behind his bride of twenty years, Joey kissed and licked neck and nibbled ear lobes, shoulder and back, then inner arms and palms and fingers. He then caressed buttocks and had his love lay on her stomach; he continued with licks and kisses down thighs and calves and engorged himself on heels and toes. Wife was quickly moist again and trembling from touch and tongue.

Lucy arose to prompt husband onto his stomach and equally worshipped him from head to toe, then massaged at prison-weary muscles until they completely yielded in relaxed-repose. Turning her lover over, she took Joey's soft manhood into her mouth. He took her womanhood into his and stretched arms and hands to caress and tease nipples again. They made love with their tongues until both groaned and twitched in ecstatic pleasure, until wife forced resistant but now hard husband to release into her willing skillful tongue-teasing mouth.

Returning to husband's mouth, wife swallowed, and kissed gently upon closed lips. Husband invited deeper. He longed for their nectars to mix. Afterward, wife moved head and body and took pillowed-repose upon the manly comfort of her man's chest. Husband held wife, stroking hair, until sleep took them into the darkness of its covered healing embrace.

The majesty of birdsong
 Calls again to me,
Awakens me and my lover
 From dreams of ecstasy

The next morning Joey stretched his awake and greeted Lucy still pillowed upon him with a warming back rub. She looked up and kissed the lips of her lover. He then ingraciously moved her off and headed to the bathroom for his bladder's necessary release. Wife followed and hugged from behind.

"Well Honey-bee, I guess I didn't need that two-by-four after all," Joey teased, gargling mouthwash at the sink.

"Always a teaser...I guess we need to get ourselves ready for the ride to Colorado?" Taking her seat, Lucy gazed in wifely affection at her wondrous lover.

Flushing, wife stood up and was arrested by powerful loaded guns into husband's embrace. He forced his minty-liquid-filled mouth upon her and squirted the minty freshness into her mouth. Lucy giggled and almost choked. Mouthwash sprayed all over the mouths, cheeks, chest and breasts of the lovers- time for another shower.

Their lovemaking this time was slower, methodical. The previous day had been impetuous, quick and carnal, but also a reserved restrained lovemaking. In truth it was. Joey fought hard not to have a premature ejaculation...several times.

This time, the man took up where he had left off fifteen years before. He had gotten his rhythm and technique back. He would spend two hours, not twenty minutes, pleasuring his love. It was worth the wait for both of them.

Showered and sexed, and sexed again and showered, by two in the afternoon the couple packed their few necessities, but left the cooler and radio.

Mounting the Chopper, Joey and Lucy headed to Colorado and home, driving straight through toward the setting sun, then by moonlight. It was a long fifteen-hour ride with more than a few stops. Joey complained a little of discomfort and fatigue, but the couple arrived safely the next afternoon at their destination.

Arriving, Joey and Lucy greeted smiling Fred, with Loretta attached at the hip, welcoming them into their furnished and well-stocked two-bedroom cabin home. Parents and grandparents, aunts and uncles, friends and other family waved from the grass clearing of the gravel horseshoe drive, but continued with their baseball game.

Thomas and Anna turned off their video game and jumped up from the couch to hug and kiss the new arrivals. Soon after separate showers, Joey and Lucy were escorted to the community hall where they enjoyed a wonderful 'welcome home' banquet and personal greetings from life-long family and friends.

＊＊＊＊＊＊＊＊＊＊

Working beside his partner on a bike Joey asked, "So Freddie-boy, how'd you get hooked up with Loretta?" Both were wearing wife-beaters, faded jeans, and work boots, with bandanas on their heads.

"You might have noticed that Henry ain't here. He has a dime to walk down in the pen. He's asked me to look after her while he's away," Fred answered honestly. He waved at Loretta and Lucy walking the long gravel circle drive.

"Brother, I do appreciate you steppin' in for me and lookin' after Lucy and Thomas, but don't you ever want to get a woman that's all your own? Don't you ever get tired of taking care of other men's wives and kids?" Joey asked, wearing a sincere and concerned expression.

"No, I really don't feel that way. The truth is Joey, you know me. You know I've always been kinda quiet and shy and a loner. Being a kind of surrogate husband and father, I got to be *you* for fifteen years. Now, I get to be Henry.

"It's the way it's been for me since I was eighteen. You know that. Sometimes it lasts a few months or years. Being with Lucy and Thomas was the longest time I've done it.

"I get the privilege to be you, to feel some of what you feel being loved by Lucy and by Thomas. And I love you man. You've been my best friend and brother since we were little squirts and terrors around here," Fred answered honestly.

Grabbing two bottles of beer from the small refrigerator nearby, Fred handed one to Joey.

"I know all that, but I just want you to have what I have...you know, forever, not just a few years," Joey confessed.

"Maybe it'll come one day. For now, I'm forty-two and Loretta will need me until I turn fifty-two. Maybe after that, I'll think about settling down," Fred advised.

The two tapped beer bottles toasting each other. Fred decided to ask humbly a question that Joey's questions had prompted.

"Joey, what would you have done if I had chosen to stay with Lucy and she would've chosen to stay with me?"

"I would've honored Lucy and your decision and headed back here alone. But I do thank you for being there for her. Women with men in prison get lonely and afraid, you know. With you there Fred, she was safe, secure, loved and cared for. I owe you man," Joey replied, thoughtfully studying his best friend's eyes.

"There was never any chance of Lucy choosing me over you, brother. Lucy has always been in love with you," Fred confessed.

Joey nodded that he knew that and toasted his friend again as Thomas, Anna, Loretta and Lucy approached.

"Joey, Anna and I have some news for you. We just told it to mama and Loretta. Anna and I are getting married. She's expecting in seven months. Dad, we would be proud and honored if you would be my best man," Thomas disclosed.

Standing, Joey shook his son's outstretched hand, hugged Anna and then his son. Fred stood up and with Lucy and Loretta created a group hug. Father looked at son with eyes brimming pride. 'Uncle' Fred's eyes teared-up, as well.

"Baby boy, as much as it would honor me to be your best man, I must decline. Here is my best man and yours. Fred is to take that honor," Joey responded.

"It would be my honor, son," Fred accepted, bear-hugging Thomas. Nearby, Anna and Lucy half-hugged

"But Son understand, you'll be sharing Fred with me," Joey disclosed.

Dropping to one knee, Joey removed his red bandana, wiped his grimy hands with it, took Lucy's left hand, kissed the modest eternal rings, and asked for her hand again in marriage.

Blushing, Lucy lifted up Joey and accepted his proposal with a prolonged hug and kiss. It was settled, they would renew their marriage vows at Thomas and Anna's wedding ceremony. Another group hug soon followed with fresh bottles of the Rocky Mountain's best beer.

The wedding ceremony was a few months later in the forest cathedral near the Trout stream just off a beautiful pristine lake. Tall pines filled with cones swaying their happy approval and applause. Birds sang as Thomas and Anna, dressed in virgin white as 'flower children', pledged their life-long love, kissed, and turned to be announced 'husband and wife'.

Soon after, father and mother, also adorned with flowered leys and wreaths, renewed their vows and kissed. Joey, smiling broadly, hugged his wife and announced that they were expecting their second child.

Family and friends, bikers all, applauded, hooped and hollered and clapped at the news. At the reception in the common hall, champagne was consumed until it ran out- not. All drank beer and whiskey happily. Only the expectant mothers declined the ministering libations due to their condition.

Fred grabbed his fiddle, Joey and Thomas their guitars, and joined their drummer Gary, their bass guitarist Stuart, with Lucy accompanying on electric piano, and performed some Credence Clearwater Revival, Eagle's hits, and other hits from the sixties and seventies. The celebration ended with Joey singing to his wife, *When you love someone,* by Bryan Adams. It was a happy time for all.

In nature's time, Thomas and Anna welcomed a baby boy into their world. He was eight-pounds-fourteen-ounces. He was beautiful, with a full head of blonde hair, fully fingered and toed with all pipes functional. He was shortly thereafter nicknamed 'the squirt'. His given name was Frederick Joseph after both of Thomas's fathers.

A few months later Lucy gave birth. She delivered a beautiful seven-pound-three-ounce baby girl. She named her daughter Clara Louise after her mother. The children would be raised as brother and sister. Joey doted on his baby daughter. Thomas tried to spoil his baby sister about as much as he did his own son.

What would have been if Joey had not made that fateful decision to mule drugs to earn illegal money to buy his loving spouse new teeth? Although time was taken from Joey and Lucy, time in the end did heal all things. The couple lived with and enjoyed their club, their extended family, children and grandchildren until their dying days.

What law could never comprehend,
What jury took from son and wife and man,
Was restored with gentle turn of hand,
By love's hourglass of healing flowing sand.

The Palomino Picnic

Eduardo was Millie's father's horseman. He was fifty now. Sadly, as a young man he had unsashed his long knife and committed an impetuous thoughtless act. Forced like a murdering Moses escaping the wrath of Pharaoh, he fled his home and country. He traveled ever north until he reached *Los Estados Unidos,* the United States.

Sergio was his given name after his father. His father was Brazilian, his mother Argentinian. Sergio senior was a gaucho, a vaquero- a cowboy- from the Patagonian grasslands that stretched, as did his extended *la familia,* from southern Brazil to Argentina. He proudly raised his five sons to be gauchos. Sergio was the eldest.

After a few years of changing his identity and working his way from one *estancia*, or cattle ranch, to another- surely siring several children along the way- saving his money, learning spoken English, 'Eduardo' ended up in southern Missouri in 1978. It was a place very far from his family and very different from his beloved *Gran Chaco*. Nevertheless, he was a free man, his own man.

Eduardo enjoyed working for Millie's father, George. He loved raising and training Quarter Horses and Palominos. He was the chief trainer. He was present for the birth of each new foal. He loved them, teased them, fussed at them, trained and rewarded them as if they were his children. In many ways they were.

Randy had known Millie since her 'tomboy' days, from Grammar School. When he turned fourteen, he summoned the courage to ask George and Margaret, Millie's mother, if he could start dating their daughter. George liked the boy and treated him like a son- he had four daughters but no sons. Instead of allowing Randy to date his eldest daughter, he allowed him to 'hang around' when he was not working on his family's farm and had Eduardo instruct him in how to train the horses- his daughter's first love.

Over his two-year apprenticeship, the boy fell more and more in love with the horses, with Eduardo, and with Millie. Eduardo adopted Randy as a son, taught him how to be a man, and shared his stories and secrets with him. He had adopted Millie as a daughter many years before.

Eduardo sported a very handsome long thick-waxed mustache that matched his long thick graying-black hair. For a middle-aged man his strength and endurance amazed everyone. He was as fit as he was when he left the *Gran Chaco*. He encouraged the skinny fourteen-year-old Randy every day to work on his puny muscles.

"What, you think these powerful creatures are going to bend to the will of a puny boy? Perhaps they will if they are in love with you. You must master them as you would a wife. Be gentle, kind, wooing them to your will and bed...but firmly, with strength.

"Powerful animals only respect strength, and they doubly respect it, as does a woman, when kindness- not cruelty- flows from that strength. Exercise your body and your brains, Randy, and the horses will follow you in-hand as will your woman."

Eduardo winked and laughed as he caressed the head of his favorite flirty girl, a year old Palomino named Delilah, feeding her an apple from his jacket pocket.

At sixteen, whether he was wearing a Cowboy hat or a Sombrero, Randy sported a manly figure. He looked and acted twenty-one. Eduardo would tease, "*La rama es ahora el arbol.*" (The twig is now the tree.) Millie had blossomed, too. She cut a fine womanly figure at fifteen that did not go unnoticed by Randy.

Eduardo many times had to caution the young man to keep his mind and eyes on the horses and not on the always-nearby 'worshiping' Millie. The warnings, though acknowledged, went unheeded. It was the bruises, bumps, cracked ribs, and a girl's amused laughter that was the young man's reward for his many obvious trespassing glances. George also took notice. It was time for *the talk*.

"Come in Randy and take a seat," George directed. Randy obeyed.

Walking up the front porch steps and through the screen door, Randy reported for work as he had done every Saturday morning for two years- his thoughts on his job and miles away from he and Millie. He dropped his hat on the nearby wicker glass covered table, took a sip from the cup of freshly brewed and poured coffee offered to him, stretched and smiled at George.

"You won't be working today, Randy. Margret and I have spoken at length to your parents about this. Everything is arranged. I have a few questions for you.

"Are you just fiddle-fartin' around here? Do you have honorable intentions toward my daughter or is your plan just to hump and dump her?" George asked this in an edgy, irritated tone.

Wearing an instant flush of red, Randy looked and felt like he had just been slapped after a harsh rebuke. He knew his heart, but he didn't know where George was coming from with the questions. He suddenly choked on his heart's fornications towards Millie and a mouth full of hot coffee. After coughing to regain his wind and composure, the boy answered humbly and honestly.

"George, I only have honorable intentions toward Millie. I love her and want to marry her once we're of age. There's no fiddle-fartin' around, sir."

"I know that son. I just wanted to get your undivided attention. Now that I have it, we need to talk man to man about your relationship with Millie.

"Millie has told me and her mother that you have begun heavy petting and that it has gotten to the groping-feeling-up grinding stage. Is that an accurate account of your amorous activities with my daughter?" George kinda looked and sounded a bit perturbed at this point.

Blushing a newer deeper shade of red, Randy added 'shocked' to his growing vocabulary of emotion. He had no 'ideal' that Millie had 'told' on them. Hell, it was her idea. She had initiated the heavy petting and foreplay, and it was all he could do to keep that wild untamed mare off his business and himself out of 'the saddle'.

"George, I meant no disrespect toward Millie. I do want to marry her one day," Randy defended, taking full responsibility for their arousing amorous activities.

"Randy, I once knew a young man like you- your age. He had a girl about Millie's age who looked just like her. She was a pretty filly- a brunette. They started dating and soon found that they couldn't wait until they were married to physically consummate their love.

"In those days it was legal, with parent's permission, to marry at sixteen. After being honest about their feelings and inability to control their passions, their parent's allowed them to marry young, and they lived with her folks until he turned eighteen and was able to rent a little cottage for them near the ranch.

"That couple was me and Millie's mother. So, I've been you. Margaret has been Millie. We know the score. We know what you're going through and have talked it over with your folks."

George seemed more composed now but Randy was sweating bullets from all pores and braced for what was to come. He knew that he and Millie were too young to marry. There was only one course of action that Millie's folks and his folks- both God-honoring church folk- to take. He would be politely asked not to see Millie again, at least until her eighteenth birthday.

Randy began to weep right there sitting on the costly wicker chair on the screened-in front porch- coughing out guilt and grief instead of coffee this time. The acre of ground before him- that led to the property line at the gravel road marked with the beginning of white-railed fence- was, like his future, unexpectedly and suddenly all-a-blur. His two years of hard work with the horses on that two-hundred acre ranch was all for naught. All that shoveling shit had turned to shit. All the time he had spent grooming his 'mare' was lost, and like his tears could never be reclaimed or replaced.

The beaten bruised heart almost exploded in the young man's aching chest. Before George could give aid and further explanation, Randy began to convulse and dry heave. It was more than he could take.

How could he be banished from his true love? How could they deprive him of her touch and not allow him to touch her again? He was truly repentant for their sins and would agree to anything...anything just to see her.

> *He wept for touch of lover lost-*
> *Hope ne'er to be regained;*
> *He wept for innocence cost-*
> *A manhood yet to be attained.*

Randy wanted to run. He wanted to run away from his fears and humiliation down that gravel driveway to the road and keep on running. "Fuck my truck," he bitterly thought. Instead of running, he glanced up at George- now hovering above him wearing an effigy of empathy- and fell to his knees. Instead of offering a eulogy for the young couple's 'once' romance, George offered a hand-up.

"Son, if I never knew that you loved my daughter before, I sure know it now. But you misread my meaning and intent. I'm not ending your romance with my daughter; I'm giving you my permission and blessing."

"What?" Randy responded in cautious-tenor, wiping his tear-filled eyes.

"Come on son; hop back up into the chair. You need to hear me out," George directed, lifting the boy up and into the wicker chair.

Randy breathed out, what he hoped would be, a long sigh of relief. With hands folded in his lap, he looked down and stretched his aching body from stiff shoulders to lanky legs. He then sat up straight resting his right boot across his left knee. George took his sheepish glance as a signal to continue their conversation.

"Son, it isn't wrong for you to love my daughter or for her to love you. It will never be wrong for you two to love each other. Margaret and I do not want you to ever feel paranoid, fearful, ashamed or guilty about expressing your love for each other. That would be the greatest sin," George stated sympathetically.

Randy had not yet fully recovered from the shame and remorse of being 'found out'. He wanted to say something but his mind was blank. He felt somewhat relieved at George's attempt to comfort, but wasn't really hearing what he was saying.

"Like I said Randy, I've been there. Millie was conceived out of wedlock because we foolishly thought we could save ourselves until we made it down the aisle to the marriage altar. But we couldn't. We got married soon after we found out that Millie was on the way.

"We felt ashamed, confused, guilty, like we had failed each other and our parents, not to mention our God. But we were in love and wanted to make it right and legal. We wanted to be a happy family, and so did our folks.

"Margaret and I never want our daughters or future son-in-laws to have to sneak around to make love to each other. We sure as hell do not want you both feeling guilty or ashamed because you have made love with each other. So, we and your parents have agreed to give our permission and blessing for your union.

"Millie's been on the pill now about six weeks. If you can promise me that you will love and cherish her until and after you are married, you may today, and hereafter, sleep with our daughter. You may have sleepovers in her bedroom and your folks have agreed that she may have sleepovers in yours.

"But that is only if you in your hearts are husband and wife. This is not for experimentation, young man. If marriage is not your goal and purpose, then you need to leave now." George got up and opened the porch screen door inviting Randy to leave...or stay.

Randy jumped up from his seat, hugged his new father-in-law, and received reassuring pats on the back. Millie's mother soon opened the front door carrying a carafe to refresh their coffees and quickly given a lift-n-twirl by her new son-in-law, followed by a hearty, "Yee-haw!"

"You've made me the happiest man alive. I will honor and cherish Millie until death do us part. I promise I will," Randy stated, wearing a relieved grin.

"We knew you would son. Mother, thank you for the refreshments, now let us men folk conclude our business," George directed his tearing wife.

Margaret withdrew back into the house.

"Your first night together should be special and neutral. We can't very well get you a motel room at your young ages, so Eduardo has offered to get a motel room for the night and loan you and Millie his cottage. You will find it clean and ready for you.

"But for your first time together, you need to think about making love to my daughter in a special place that is only known to the two of you. It's important to create special memories. That cannot be your bedroom or hers, or even Eduardo's cottage. Do you have a place like that, son?

"There's a place about a mile from my folks' house down by the creek. I spray it every so often, like I do the lawn around the house, to kill ticks and chiggers.

"But that's not the place. Not far from there is a little secluded spot on the creek where my dad built me a tree house.

"I was eight at the time and helped him. It has three stories with a lookout at the top. Up until I was twelve, I could stand up in the first floor. Now, I have to stoop quite a bit. But the place has many fond memories for me. I'd like that to be our place. I'd like our first time to be there by the creek and maybe in the tree house," Randy disclosed, blushing a little grin.

"Son, it sounds like the perfect place. It's only three miles to your folk's farm. Why don't you saddle up the Palominos and take the picnic brunch Margret has prepared for you," George recommended.

The men shook hands again and Randy was off to saddle up Delilah and her Palomino partner, the handsome Samson.

****

When the young man returned to the house riding Samson- Delilah in tow- he found a smiling Millie on the front porch with picnic basket that he 'hitched' to his saddle horn. Randy then lashed the extra blankets behind the saddle with the saddlebags.

After hugging and kissing Millie's folks, the couple galloped down the gravel drive and then trotted down the road a few miles until they reached a gate that led to an open fallow field. Beyond in the distance just over a gentle sloping hill was a treeline and with it, the meandering creek. Randy dismounted, opened the gate, led the horses and his love through, shut and secured it, and followed the 'shortcut' dirt road.

Arriving at their destination, Randy assisted Millie in her dismount, took one of the blankets from atop his saddlebag and unrolled it on the grassy ground near the creek. Millie unlashed the picnic basket and laid out their feast. Randy took the six-pack of soft drinks and secured them behind tree roots under the water to keep them cool. When he returned, Millie was pouring orange juice into plastic cups.

Scratching his cheek, Randy teasingly said, "Well, I guess this is one way to get a day off from work; I hope it's with pay."

"If you'd rather, I can pack all this up and we can go back home. I'm sure my dad can find something for you to do," Millie teased back.

"Nope, I think I've got enough work around here to keep me busy for a spell; I got me a mare to break," Randy double-teased.

Taking Millie into his arms, Randy kissed her deeply but differently. It was not the initiation of heavy petting in a secret place- the beginning of guilty pleasures in a stolen moment. Both instantly felt, knew that it was husband and wife at the beginning of foreplay- freely giving, freely accepting, and freely expressing their love.

Within seconds, the food was forgotten. Randy let go his bride, retrieved the two other rolled blankets from atop his saddlebags, and threw them over his shoulders. He led Millie to the great oak tree of his youth nearby and up the nailed-on ladder rungs to the hatch beneath the first floor. He pushed the hinged-hatch open, and once in and on his knees, lifted his love through the threshold of it.

Millie knew that her beloved was a strong strapping fella. With the lift came new respect for that strength. Again, she found herself in strong arms and deeply kissed with her hands locked behind the muscular tanned neck. Blankets thoughtlessly tossed to the floor, now spread one on top of the other, foreshadowing what must come- one lover atop the other.

With gentlest intent and action, lover undressed lover —hats and boots, the first articles to go. Then big buckled belts, and finally the clothes were shed. When down to briefs, bra, and panties, you would think the modest lovers would have paused and studied each other a minute or two. After all, they had never been in such a state of undress in front of each other.

They did pause and study...for about three seconds. Then both willfully and quickly shed those nuisances to novice lovemaking. In each other's arms again, on their knees Randy and Millie kissed deeply.

Although instructed by her mother in the art of first lovemaking and knowing of a young man's difficulties in holding on to his 'load', Millie found herself a blank slate. Randy, not yet instructed on how to make love to a woman, had driven all thoughts out of her head with one long deep kiss.

As his member stood alert and erect and throbbed for release at Millie's first touch, Randy let out a gasp and kissed more deeply. She responded by pulling him to her tightly. Feeling her warm 'cunny' on his tingling ball sack, he could not help it.

With muscled horse-tamer hands, Randy grabbed and pulled Millie's buttocks tight. It was as if he was pulling the reins of a Palomino at full gallop, trying to arrest or at least slow his coming release. The cowboy soon learned his first lesson in trying to make love with an untrained teenage prick.

As Randy exploded onto his lower torso and Millie felt her love's warm load empty first upon her stomach then shoot higher, she facilitated and pulled Randy in even tighter. He kissed her mouth then neck, and then wept into it. He felt so ashamed. He had ruined their first time together.

Millie kissed comfort into her love beginning at mouth then down to nipples and rock hard abs. Then she got a little freaky and caught Randy so unawares that she once again took his breath away. She licked his load and then took his throbbing member into her mouth and began to twirl her tongue around and around, remembering some of what her mother had instructed her to do.

What should have been an act performed pre-ejaculative, was being performed post-ejaculative. Neither had any idea of what that meant or how it would feel. Randy gasped and groaned at first at the amazing tingling trauma he was experiencing. Then he grabbed Millie's head.

Millie thought that her lover was 'getting more into it'. But he was just trying to get out of it. The tingling trauma was too much, too intense, and it hurt. He pulled his lover's tongue and head off him.

Looking down in shock, dismay, and some discomfort, Randy wondered what to say or do next. He was not in the mood now for anything except maybe a wash-up. Millie was in the mood for much more.

"Mills, um...thank you? Um, that was great, really. I am really sorry for that. I don't know what happened.

Well, I do know what happened; I was there when it happened. I'm so sorry," Randy begged, tears filling his eyes again.

Millie arose and kissed her love with cum-softened lips.

It was a salty kiss, for sure. That kiss made Randy feel even more awkward. He had not tasted his own sperm since his first time- his first wet dream at the age of thirteen. He only did it then to see what it tasted like. It was not as if he had made a habit of tasting it.

Millie hugged her hubby, beginning to adopt his awkward feelings. She did not know what to do either. Doubts flooded her mind. She hoped that Randy was not going to ejaculate prematurely every time they endeavored to make love. Nevertheless, she pushed those thoughts aside.

Her mother had told her this might happen. It had happened to George the first time he and Margaret made love, but her dad had lasted seven minutes and did manage to ejaculate into her mother's vagina. That's was the story of Millie's conception, as they recalled it for her.

'What to do, what to do?' Millie mulled over in her mind. Randy pulled her in more tightly and rubbed her back. He didn't know what to do either.

"Hungry?" Millie asked, looking up at her beloved.

"Starved," Randy happily replied.

"I've got a bandana in my back jean pocket. Let me just wipe us clean," Millie offered.

After the cursory cleaning, Randy stated, "Wife, you missed some cum under your right tit."

"They're called 'breasts', Randy," Millie corrected, as she lifted her right breast to wipe it clean.

"Ok. Millie dear, you had some cum under your right tittie-breast," Randy responded, laughing as he took his left hand and playfully bounced the right boob up and down several times.

"Thank you husband," Millie replied.

She grinned back, shaking her head thinking, 'If that's all it takes to amuse my man...' Randy then slipped on his jeans and Millie her jeans and blouse and descended the tree house.

Shirtless and bootless, Randy ate his egg and bacon sandwiches and drank his orange juice. Millie did the same. Neither spoke a word. Finally, realizing that he was 'the man of the house', Randy spoke his mind.

"Mills, I am so sorry for disappointing you. I didn't know I'd cum like that, so quick. I just got really excited at seeing you and feeling you for the first time. I'm good to go again, if you're ready. Got any suggestions," Randy begged in an unintentional but sexy baritone.

"Baseball...that's what my dad says he thinks about to keep himself from releasing early," Millie responded.

"It is a slow mostly boring game. Can you be more specific?"

"My daddy says that the man plays all the positions but catcher. I'm the catcher; you're the pitcher and batter mostly. He says that when you're pitchin' and at bat- when you're feeling that you want to swing hard and hit a homer- that you should step back out of the batter's box a minute," Millie offered, recalling what her mother had told her about her father's recipe for long-lasting lovemaking.

"That sounds like good advice, really. I never would've equated making love to baseball. What else did your dad say?"

"He said that making love should go the full nine-innings and into overtime if you can manage it. He said it takes a lot of practice. But the batter is to work hard at waiting to hit that big home run until the catcher is ready for it," Millie further advised.

"But the batter and catcher are on different teams. Why would the catcher be just as ready and excited for the home run of his opponent? That doesn't really make sense, does it?" Randy inquired, scratching the day growth of beard on his chin and neck.

"Honey, you're missing the point. The catcher is a girl, me. And you better be glad I am on a different team, if you get my meaning. Your job is to pitch and pitch, swing and swing, until I am ready for you to hit the home run. And if you haven't figured it out yet, the batter's box is my pussy and the home run is my orgasm," Millie enlightened.

A light bulb went on in Randy's head. He suddenly looked amazed and pleased.

"Got it; like the catcher in baseball, you're going to signal me what pitch you think I ought to throw and I'll nod that I got it. You signal me and I'll throw the pitches you tell me throw. Then when you've had enough of my pitching and swinging, I hit that home run ball.

"Play ball!'" Randy shouted, lifting Millie off the picnic blanket.

Thrusting her onto his shoulder, husband carried wife to their honeymoon nest in the great oak tree of sweet childhood memory- now a place that would be even sweeter and dearer than before.

The ball players' second attempt at lovemaking lasted about 90 minutes and was equally exciting for both the pitcher-batter and the catcher. The pitcher did have to retire from the batter's box more than a few times during those nine innings of play. Nevertheless, Randy did hit that home run ball right there in the batter's box to Millie's delight.

Afterward, Randy led Millie down the creek bank until they came upon the swimming hole. There they swung from a rope and branch-jumped into the cool waters, swam naked, and then sunbathed on the nearby sandy-dirt shore. It was not long before foreplay began and lovemaking followed. Randy's stamina and enthusiasm that day would never be forgotten by Millie, and she had the inner thigh bruises to prove it. (He would complain of a sore and tender penis for a few days and wear a condom during lovemaking to allow for healing.)

About four that afternoon, the couple rode to Randy's parents' farmhouse where they presented themselves as husband and wife and enjoyed a wonderful supper. All present beamed with pride. The only tense moment came when Randy's parents, Bob and Joy, cautioned the couple not to tell even close friends about 'the arrangement'.

"We might get excommunicated from the Baptist Church, Son, if the pastor finds out; and that is rare indeed," Joy forewarned.

"Mom, don't worry. We won't even tell our best friends," Randy assured, side hugging her.

He and Millie kissed his folks goodbye, mounted Samson and Delilah and rode to spend the night in their honeymoon cottage. Dusk was approaching.

****

As the couple arrived at the ranch house, the front porch light came on and George and Margaret descended the stairs with Eduardo. Kisses and congratulations offered, mother escorted daughter into the house to prepare for the honeymoon night and to hear about her afternoon delights.

George shook Randy's hand and sat on the front porch to smoke a cigar and drink a little bourbon. Eduardo took Samson and Delilah in hand and led them and Randy to the stables. He wanted to hear about the lovebirds activities that afternoon and to give fatherly counsel on the night to come as they unsaddled and groomed the horses and bedded them down for the night.

After hearing a brief and blushing play-by-play of Randy and Millie's amorous activities, Eduardo laughed and patted the young man several times on both shoulders. He too beamed pride, but then sobered up to give advice.

"So, did you both also use your tongues in your lovemaking?"

"Si Eduardo, we used our tongues. But it was mostly Millie who did that. Like I said, after I came prematurely the first time, she licked me and sucked me until it hurt. I had to stop her," Randy confessed.

"And how was it when you tasted her cunny? Did she not open as a flower to you? Did she not groan and tremble in ecstasy?"

"But Eduardo, I never put my tongue in her cunny, only my fingers. She never told me to do that. You see, she is the catcher and I'm the pitcher. She never signaled me to do that to her," Randy confessed, looking a little embarrassed and confused.

"Oh son, you denied her one of the greatest of pleasures. Your tongue should tease and tickle her until she becomes as moist as the morning dew. You must eat from her garden tonight. It will be a wonderful surprise for her, no?" Eduardo counseled, stroking his waxed mustache.

"And I would do this sometime during our foreplay?" asked Randy, fishing in Eduardo's eyes for the answer he sought.

"*Exactemente*," Eduardo replied, sympathetically, "it will quicken her orgasm...and your home run."

Walking up to the cottage Randy asked, "I guess you're leaving now for the motel?"

"Si, I am leaving now. The cottage and bedroom is prepared for you. Don't worry. Your job is to give pleasure until her orgasm, mi amigo.

"Thrust more upward than down when in missionary position, unless she tells otherwise; good luck," wished Eduardo.

Taking his overnight bag, the old gaucho stepped off the front porch. He paused only long enough to advise, "Don't worry, Randy. Sleep in and make love again in the morning. I won't come knocking at the door until near church time."

Randy let out his second long sigh of relief. For some reason he suddenly felt nervous. He looked every bit the novice bridegroom that he was. He quickly smelled his underarms. He was pitting badly, but had no time to wash up.

It was time to man-up; the training wheels were off. No premature ejaculation, no foul balls this time would be tolerated. This time had to be perfect; it was their honeymoon night.

Seeing his beautiful bride approach should have melted all nervousness into firm resolve, but it caused the bridegroom to sweat even more. All he could think about was his stink and the fact that he had no 'ideal' how to perform cunnilingus.

Trying to look and feel in control, Randy stepped off the porch and escorted Millie onto it. She smelled nice; she had had a douche and shower, he could tell. He smelled like...horse, or worse.

"You sure smell nice, Mills," Randy nervously stated, opening the front door of the cottage for his love.

"Aren't you forgetting something, Randy?" Millie asked.

"Right...I'm sorry baby; I had to groom and bed down the horses. I haven't had the time to bathe," Randy acknowledged, sweating now from all pores.

"No silly; aren't you going to carry me over the threshold?"

"Oh, right...sorry Mills; surely."

Randy scooped up his bride, whisked her across the threshold, and dropped her just on the other side of it. He closed the door, slid his hands into his back pockets and looked sheepishly down at his bride. Millie began wondering if he was waiting for some kind of reward for chivalry.

Glancing around the room wearing a smirk of a smile, the boy commented, "Well, I guess the place looks clean and nice."

"Yes, it does," Millie responded, also looking around the room.

"Music- that's what we need. Want to do some dancin'?" Randy offered.

"Sure. Wonder what kind of music Eduardo has in his collection?" Millie wondered aloud.

Walking over to a table holding the stereo with a crate holding LP albums, Randy and Millie thumbed and thumbed finding only albums of Mariachi bands. They paused a moment to gaze into each other's eyes and grinned.

"I guess we'll be makin' our own music tonight," Randy observed.

"After I give you a bath, mister," Millie advised.

Taking Randy's hand, she led him into the bathroom off the bedroom.

The bath was an unexpected pleasure for Randy. He had not been given a bath by anyone since he was a baby and little boy. He especially liked it when Millie took extra time to clean his genitals.

Rubbing that rough washcloth on the head of his dick was pure heaven for him. He groaned and stretched himself long in the old claw bathtub and begged her to do it again and again. She giggled at him and complied.

By the time the bath was over, Randy had splashed Millie soaked-n-wet, and she had stripped and joined him. It was their first bath together, and they reveled in the slippery soapy sexy suds. 'It's much better than making dry and sweaty love,' Randy would later reflect.

Plug chain found
By tickling playful toes,
Water swirls down
Leaving lovers in repose

The couple was not long in bed until cunnilingus became the hallmark of Randy's forte of lovemaking. Millie in fact was so aroused that she almost hit a homerun before the pitcher even had a chance to pitch or swing. Actually, baseball was the farthest thing from their minds.

Wife decided to share with husband the bliss she was experiencing. As Millie removed herself from Randy's magnificent mouth and moved into a sixty-nine position, his suddenly disappointed and dumbfounded expression transformed into a broad manly-proud smile. He continued his tongue's expedition of erotic discovery on and about the clitoris.

Millie's erotic enthusiasm soon left Randy as breathless as he had left her a few minutes earlier. It wasn't long before he found himself breathless again, but not in a good way. As these things tend to go with novice love-makers, now and then, there is an unintentional trespass, and Millie had committed it.

"Damn baby, what are you doing down there?" Randy groaned out all of a sudden. He knew what she was doing and did not like it one bit.

"I'm just nibbling on your nuts," Millie playfully replied.

Grabbing her head and removing his loins far from it, Randy gave a disparaging look in Millie's general direction. She immediately noted that his face was beet-red, his eyes tearing.

"Did I do anything wrong, honey?" Millie asked, sitting up.

"Mills, I don't want to sound cruel or ungrateful, but...surely God is merciful enough that the fires of eternal torment don't hurt like that," Randy declared, rubbing his offended appendages, tears now flooding his eyes.

"But you nibbled on my nipples and on my vagina, why can't I nibble on your nuts?" Millie asked defensively.

She felt somewhat offended and put-off at her lover's extreme characterization of her attempts to playfully please him.

"Mills baby, you can nibble all over a man, but not there. The testicles are the most sensitive part of a man.

"You just don't chew on 'em. Did your mother tell you to do that?" Randy responded.

"No, I just thought of it. I'm sorry. It won't happen again," Millie apologized.

Wife scooted up to her wounded lover and sympathetically removed his protective hands and replaced them with her own. It was not long before her gentle tongue replaced them, and Randy was happily relieved again. He returned to Millie's garden and continued cunnilingus until she had her first orgasm of the night. He held off hitting his homerun ball until well after midnight, just before they surrendered to sleep.

****

There have never been two happier or sleepier sinners in church. After a wonderful late breakfast, Randy and Millie joined her folks to attend the morning Methodist church service. They smiled and winked and fingered each other's hands throughout the late morning. Thankfully, the service only lasted an hour- not like the Baptist service that Randy was used to that lasted almost two hours.

After a hearty 'home cooked' meal in town at a small café near the church, Millie and her family and beau returned home. Randy took off his church clothes, donned work clothes, and caught up on his chores at the ranch. Millie helped her mother strip the cottage bed and replaced the sheets with clean ones. Eduardo returned from the motel to a clean and sanitary house. However, he would never again look at his bachelor bed the same way.

****

The summer of Millie's eighteenth birthday, she and Randy wed in a service down at the creek where the family picnicked. Over one-hundred attended that June day. Folding chairs and tables were borrowed from the Methodist church. It was a beautiful service.

Randy's two older brothers were his groomsmen. His friend, Greg, was his best man. Millie's sisters were her bridesmaids. A dance followed at the church's fellowship hall.

Using a portion of their savings and the generous gifts from their folks, friends and relatives, the couple honeymooned for a week in Hawaii. On the flight from St. Louis to L.A. and then on to Hawaii, Millie read a few short fantasy novels that she purchased at a Lambert Airport gift shop. They were about wizards, elves, and damsels in distress. She instantly fell in love with the medieval romantic genre.

In Hawaii, after site-seeing and swimming, and wonderful dinners, the couple would return to their hotel room and make love, but before retiring for the night, they would read to each other from the fantasy novels. Randy too fell in love with the stories.

Once back home, they purchased more, read and enjoyed them nightly. Soon they were role-playing with Randy becoming R'Andy the Wizard who would rescue, woo, and win his damsel in distress, M'Illie, with his *magic wand*. It was a wonderful time for them.

During Randy and Millie's third year of marriage, twin boys were born to them. They were handsome like their father. Uncle Eduardo offered that one should be named Edward and the other Sergio. Millie wanted to name the eldest George after her father, and the younger, Robert after Randy's father. Therefore, the eldest ended up with the name George Edward, the younger, Robert Sergio.

Soon after, Randy purchased a doublewide trailer and placed it near his family's farmhouse. Although Millie and the boys did spend most days at her parent's house at the ranch, nights spent at the trailer or at Randy's parent's house. It was during their fourth year of marriage that trouble visited them.

Unable to secure further bank loans to operate the farm and to pay personal expenses, Bob and Joy would soon have to give up the farm and move into town. This devastated all, but especially Randy and Millie- they could not lose their special place. They had to do something. George and Margaret had their heads above water, but just barely. Mortgaged from hoof-to-hilt too, they could not offer aid.

Randy confided in his best friend, Greg, and together they came up with a plan that had to work. They would use some of the acreage near the woods- far from roads and spying eyes- and grow marijuana. Randy had come to enjoy the mellowing weed and readily agreed to the business plan.

It was to be a very profitable endeavor, and would have been, if they had not been found out by a game warden. A hopeless time became even more hopeless. The farm was lost and auctioned off; Millie and the boys moved in with her mom and dad. Randy and Greg got ten years.

Randy's departure was sad, as you can imagine, and filled with promises of fidelity from husband and wife. George was angry but his sad disappointment in his son-in-law melted away due to his love for him, his daughter, and grandsons. Regret and grief was the daily food the extended family ate for seven and one-half years. That was when the paroled-release came and Randy returned home.

****

As Eduardo drove his silent reflective son home, they turned off the highway onto a blacktop road that soon became gravel. Although he knew it would cause Randy more than a little grief, he drove down the gravel road that ran parallel to the young man's once-upon-a-time family farm. The young man, now over thirty but looking none-the-worse-for-wear, wept as he glanced at his childhood home and the doublewide in the distance. Eduardo did not slow down; he squeezed Randy's shoulder and kept driving.

Expecting that their next stop would be George's ranch, Randy was surprised when Eduardo turned his Chevy pickup onto the 'short cut' dirt road that led to his and Millie's special place by the creek. Before he could ask what was going on, Eduardo exited the pickup but did not unlock the gate. He made a phone call on his cellular.

Making his apologies, Eduardo left the young man and his modest bag of belongings at the gate and drove away. His only instructions "Wait here."

Feeling abandoned, Randy looked around in all directions. The field lay fallow once again. The wind blew briskly against his skin. He was a cowboy without a horse or hat or boots. Thankfully, Eduardo had brought him a Levi shirt and jeans to wear home but no belt.

Randy wanted to fall to his knees and kiss the dirt. He was home, but then realized that he wasn't. This land was not and never would be his. It had been forfeited to the bank and probably auctioned for pennies on the dollar. His eyes filled with regretful tears.

As the young man wondered why he was ditched at that gate, he was tempted to walk down the rutted dirt road to the creek. Surely, his tree house love nest was still there. But prison had destroyed his dreams and even the desire to relive them in memory. It was all a dead past never to be reclaimed, so why bother to think about it. Randy turned from facing the 'creek' direction and looked the opposite way toward more of the land his family had lost.

Fifteen minutes elapsed but the young man felt like it had been hours. He knelt down then sat down by the old gatepost that his grandfather had set many years before.

He took a weed into his mouth and began chewing it for its bitter-sweetness.

"What the fuck is goin' on?" Randy mumbled to himself.

Looking around again, he felt not like the 'tree' he once was. "Eduardo, I am in no mood for a joke," the 'twig' further complained.

Just then, Randy heard the soft sound of approaching hoof beats. Standing up, he listened and looked in the direction of the road leading to the ranch. The sound was coming from behind him. Turning, he could not believe his eyes or ears. There was Millie riding graceful Delilah with faithful Samson in tow. She dismounted and ran toward her one and only love.

Suddenly the twig became the tree again. Randy quickly opened the gate. The couple kissed and kissed, hugged and hugged and wept seven and one-half years of relieved tears. Millie then secured the gate and led her husband by hand to Samson.

"You do remember how to mount and ride a horse?" Millie teased.

"You bet your sweet ass I do. How come you're coming from the creek, Mills? It ain't ours no more," Randy commented regretfully.

"Just follow me down the road to just over the horizon," Millie tempted then galloped away.

Randy pursued his love at a gentle gallop until he had caught her up just at the top of the gently sloping hill. Just over it, he spied a sight that, at first, didn't register. It was out of place, unfamiliar. What was he seeing in the distance near their secret spot?

"Welcome home Randy," Millie greeted, holding onto her saddle horn, standing up in the stirrups.

There in the distance was a doublewide stationed near the creek but on newly elevated land close to the great Oak of his boyhood tree house. There was a gravel drive coming into it from the north- from the ranch. Pickup trucks a-plenty and a Cadillac were parked out front. There was also a large storage shed.

"What does this all mean, Mills?" Randy asked as his eyes brimmed anew, but this time with thankful prophetic tears.

"We weren't able to save your family's home or most of the land. But Eduardo had enough money saved to where he could buy at auction the twenty acres bordering dad's ranch including our special place. Our special place is now our home," Millie disclosed with revelatory thankful tears.

Randy moved Samson closer to Delilah and ahorseback gave his wife a gentle hug and kiss. After, they rode on to the trailer. Beyond it, by the creek, folding tables were set up and covered with fried chicken, barbequed ribs and baked beans, coleslaw, potato salad, corn on the cob, corn bread, sweet rolls, iced tea, cakes, pies, homemade ice cream- it was a true family reunion and welcome home. Randy and Millie's parents welcomed their son with hugs and kisses, as did Eduardo and half the county.

The twins, now eight, hugged their father and chided him for his *uncowboyly* attire. Millie quickly remedied the humiliation fetching her man's boots, hat and silver-plated buckled belt. The festivities went on until the sweet tea and cold beer ran out, until leftovers found their way into the overstuffed refrigerator of the doublewide. Friends and family left for home basking in the blissful joy shinning from their host's faces.

Before Eduardo departed for his cottage, Randy bear hugged him promising to pay back every penny for the property and trailer. Eduardo would not hear of it. Besides, George and Margaret had already done that. There was only one payment that anyone wanted from Randy.

"Just promise to keep your nose clean and love your woman and children like they deserve to be loved," Eduardo counseled.

"I will; I promise- no more pot, no more crazy plans to get rich. All I want is what I always wanted, to be a good husband to Mills and a good father to my boys," Randy replied.

Eduardo bear hugged Randy again and left in his Chevy pickup. Millie, just returning to the yard after putting the boys in bed, came from behind and entwined her long fingers into her husbands. Not able to be anybody but himself, Randy initiated their night of lovemaking with heartfelt but unnecessary tearful apologies.

"Millie, I am so sorry for all I've put you through. As God as my witness, I will never do anything to jeopardize you or the boys or do anything to hurt you ever again. Can you forgive me for my stupidity?"

"Well, you did only make it through the tenth grade...I have to take that into consideration. However, you did earn your G.E.D. in prison, so I expect you not to be nearly as stupid in the future," Millie replied.

"I do have my G.E.D. There is that. And I do still love you with all my heart and want to spend the rest of my days making love to you...if you'll have me," Randy responded, unable to stop the flow of tender tears.

"Randy, it was never wrong for me to love you, and I always will."

Wife took husband's strong right forearm into hers and walked him into their new love nest. There, in their bed, they made tender love for many years and asked Eduardo's advice in the naming of three more children- two girls and a boy. And, by the way, Randy never did commit the sin of not loving Millie.

With repented crimes in quick retreat,
Faithful wife embraced and kids at feet,
The cowboy's life became complete
In a doublewide near childhood's creek.

Postscripts

Elements of stories float freely in my head,
Yet to be interwoven thread upon bare thread;
Jig Saw puzzle pieces bounce around there too,
Fleeing dark corners until the writing's through.
****

The reader may now, with my earnest urging
And gifts serendipitous, if not divine,
Depart these pages to weave their own stories
Taking common threads from mine.

I bow to you, my fellow and future Word Weavers.
The Author

The spirit of the Lord GOD is upon me,
Because the LORD has anointed me;
He has sent me to bring glad tidings to the lowly,
To heal the brokenhearted,
To proclaim liberty to the captives and
Release to the prisoners,
To announce a year of favor from the LORD
And a day of vindication by our God,
To comfort all who mourn;
To place on those who mourn in Zion
A diadem instead of ashes,
To give them oil of gladness in place
Of mourning,
A glorious mantle
Instead of a listless spirit.
They will be called oaks of justice,
Planted by the LORD to show his glory.

Isaiah 61:1-3 The New American Bible

Contact the author at:
mvrae@outlook.com

Printed in Great Britain
by Amazon